Bede's Life of

St Cuthbert

In a Modern English Version

by Simon Webb

Published by the Langley Press, Durham, 2016

The cover shows St Cuthbert in a boat at sea, from
Chapter XI of Bede's Prose Life of St Cuthbert:
illuminated manuscript from the last quarter
of the twelfth century

(British Library Yates Thompson MS 26)
www.bl.uk

This book is dedicated to my mother,
Barbara Irene Webb

Contents

Seated Scribe: From BL Yates Thompson MS 26

Introduction

Some time around the middle of the eleventh century AD, a priest called Aelfrid arrived at the monastery at Jarrow. He was there to keep his annual vigil by the tomb of a monk who had died there three centuries earlier. Aelfrid's vigil always happened on May the twenty-sixth, the anniversary of the monk's death.

One year, Aelfrid was not to be found in the church or monastery of Jarrow on the morning after his vigil. His companions, who had no doubt been expecting to accompany him back to Durham, had no idea where he was, and were surprised at his absence. When Aelfrid didn't appear the next year, and when, as the twelfth-century chronicler Simeon of Durham put it, he 'conducted himself like a person who had secured the object of his desires,' some of the Jarrow monks must have concluded that Aelfrid had stolen one of their greatest treasures – the bones of the Venerable Bede.

Bede's bones were worth Aelfrid's attention, because the memory of this monk, who lived in a savage age, in a remote part of the north of England, was revered in his own time, and throughout the Middle Ages.

Bede was not only a monk, but also a priest, a

poet, a historian, an educator, a linguist and translator, and what we would now call a scientist. His life and works are among the glittering treasures of the Northumbrian Golden Age, which some have called the Northumbrian Renaissance, although it happened some six centuries before the Renaissance of the late Middle Ages. Like the proverbial 'Renaissance man', Bede was skilled in many different areas.

A resident of the combined monastery of Wearmouth-Jarrow, Bede wrote on the Bible and theology, on the reckoning of time, on the Holy Land, and most notably on the history of his own people – the Angles, or English. His *Ecclesiastical History*, completed in 731, stretches from Roman times to his own period, is constantly in print in many different languages, and is still a vital source of information for historians.

As well as being a monk, priest and scholar, Bede is regarded by Roman Catholics as a Doctor of the Church, and by both Anglicans and Catholics as a saint.

It seems that the subtle Aelfrid, who transferred Bede's bones under cover of darkness, was in the habit of 'collecting' the relics of local saints and placing them in or near the tomb of the greatest northern saint of all – St Cuthbert, who died on the twentieth of March, 687 AD.

Aelfrid seems to have felt that he had a special connection with this saint, as Cuthbert, though long dead, regularly told him what to do. Aelfrid even possessed a hair of the saint, which is said to have had miraculous properties. If placed over hot coals, the hair would not burn as one would expect an ancient hair to do: instead it glowed like a piece of gold wire.

This miraculous hair was found when Cuthbert's tomb was opened in 1827: it turned out to be an actual piece of gold wire.

After frequent questioning, Aelfrid admitted that the bones of Bede were indeed in Cuthbert's tomb, but he doesn't seem to have confessed to actually stealing them: he merely said that nobody knew better than he did, where the body in question was.

Simeon tells us that Bede's bones may have been those found later, in Cuthbert's tomb, in a little linen bag.

If the means by which Bede's bones ended up in Durham Cathedral seem a little shady, the answer to the question of why Cuthbert's body lies there involves the re-telling of an epic tale, with some bizarre and miraculous elements.

Like Bede, Cuthbert didn't start his long sleep in Durham, which would have been an insignificant little place in Anglo-Saxon times. As Bede's *Prose Life of St Cuthbert* relates, the saint died on the island of Inner Farne, and his body was quickly transported for burial on the neighbouring island of Lindisfarne.

There it rested for as long as a century and a half, before the threat of Viking raids persuaded Bishop

Egcred that Cuthbert's body, and also the living monks of Lindisfarne, should leave their island. There then followed a period of some hundred and sixty years during which Cuthbert's body rested at various places, including Norham on the River Tweed, Whithorn in Galloway, Crayke in Yorkshire and Chester-le-Street to the north of Durham; before it came to rest in Durham itself.

Not all the dates in this history can be known for sure, but it is likely that it was some sixty years later when the light-fingered Aelfrid added Bede's remains to those of Cuthbert, who already shared his tomb with pieces of Saint Aidan and Saint Oswald.

That Bede and Cuthbert now lie at opposite ends of Durham Cathedral is something that might have pleased Bede, since he seems to have had a deep devotion to Cuthbert, who died when Bede was a child.

Among his numerous other writings, Bede wrote no less than three biographies of his fellow-Northumbrian: the prose life included in his *Ecclesiastical History*, a biography in the form of a poem, and the prose biography, a version of which is printed below.

The Cuthbert Bede presents in his *Prose Life of St Cuthbert* is a picture of a Christian who is absolutely perfect, according to Bede's criteria, which are of course the criteria of a monk of eighth-century Northumbria.

Bede's Cuthbert has qualities that are still

admired in many cultures: he is kind and courteous, caring about both people and animals, physically brave and hardy, patient, honest, wise, well-read, cheerful and hospitable, a good friend, and a good teacher and public speaker. He also has a number of useful practical skills: he is able to put up buildings for himself on his island hermitage (admittedly with the help of angels), he is able to raise barley there, and he had experience of working as a shepherd.

This last skill was no trifling thing in those times, when British sheep were liable to be taken not just by rustlers, but by wolves and perhaps even bears. Practical work was an important part of life in a monastery as well as life as a hermit in those days, and Bede tells us that Cuthbert would enthusiastically work with his hands, just like the other monks.

Cuthbert is also quite lacking in the qualities that continue to ruin many personalities today. He has little or no trace of those notorious seven deadly sins, first enumerated by Gregory the Great, who died some thirty years before Cuthbert was born. In Bede's pages, the saint exhibits little or no personal pride or greed, has no interest in women (or men) as objects of physical desire, doesn't seem to envy anyone, has a very modest appetite for food, and speaks and acts calmly and patiently in situations where other men would show anger.

His attitude to the remaining deadly sin, sloth or laziness, takes us into an area where Bede's Cuthbert acts in ways that most modern people would find at best eccentric, and at worst reckless, even insane.

Bede's book is full of examples of Cuthbert deliberately depriving himself of sleep, usually to spend nights on end in prayer or in the singing of psalms.

It is interesting that this ability to go without sleep is also something that devotees of Buddhism have tried to obtain. Legendary stories about the Chinese monk Bodhidharma, who may have lived a century or two before Cuthbert, state that he sometimes went without sleep for years on end, and that he cut off his own eyelids to stop himself dozing off.

Bede's Cuthbert seems to have regarded sleep as a dangerous temptation, an invitation to slothful habits, and thus a snare of the devil. By the same token, the ability to go without sleep is seen by Bede as a pious, even a miraculous characteristic. One of Cuthbert's first great visionary experiences happens during a night when he is awake and praying, surrounded by his sleeping companions. After that experience, he laments the fact that most people sleep at night, and risk missing the nocturnal activities of angels.

Bede's book is rather contradictory in this regard, however. Some of the sick people who are miraculously cured by Cuthbert fall into long, deep sleeps before they wake up, free of their illness. This suggests that Bede knew that under some circumstances sleep, which Shakespeare calls 'Nature's soft nurse', could be very beneficial.

A cynic might say that Cuthbert's sleeplessness, which Bede himself tried to imitate in his own life, was a contributory factor to his early death (he probably died in his early fifties) and was the reason why he saw visions and heard voices. Modern experiments with sleep deprivation have seen test subjects experiencing visual and auditory hallucinations. Cuthbert's Christian cast of mind would surely have led him to interpret hallucinations as messages from God, some of which prophesied future events. The demons Cuthbert is supposed to have banished from his island may also have been hallucinations.

The habit of 'watching' or going without sleep was one ingredient in the asceticism, or deliberate hard living, which was engaged in by Christian monks, hermits, anchorites and others in this period, especially those who were influenced by the Celtic Christian tradition. These people would also deny themselves adequate food and warm shelter, would often cut themselves off from human contact, and refuse wine and beer, preferring water.

The most extreme example of Cuthbert's asceticism recorded by Bede is his habit of praying while immersed in the North Sea, at night. This would have been dangerous, and not just for his future health: he could easily have been washed out to sea and drowned.

Another aspect of the asceticism of Cuthbert and some of his peers is their attitude to illness. They welcomed illness as a test from God which, if they passed it, would increase their merit in God's eyes and guarantee them a place in heaven.

Cuthbert himself seems to have stopped short of deliberately courting illness for its own sake, but his hard-living, and his practice of touring his diocese when there was a visitation of the plague, tend to suggest that he certainly wasn't afraid of getting ill.

It may be, of course, that he believed he was immune to the plague, as he had recovered from it earlier in life: and we can't really accuse him of deliberately shortening his life, as the early fifties was a ripe old age at which to die in Anglo-Saxon times: archaeological evidence suggests that many people died in their thirties.

Cuthbert's deliberate hard living must have made him feel very uncomfortable at times, but even on warm days, when he'd allowed himself to eat a decent meal, he may still have felt discomfort because of the disease that afflicted him for most of his life.

Bede tells us about a nasty tumour on his knee, and that, when he later recovered from the plague, the pestilence somehow settled in his bowels, and remained with him. Dr Selby Plummer, a local Durham medic who examined the evidence in 1899, suspected that the saint might never have had the plague at all, and that when he came down with tuberculosis, the doctors thought he had plague because it was a plague year, and so many other people had it.

The fact that Cuthbert's swellings often occurred

at his joints; as well as his appearance, his tendency to cry, and his visions, all seemed to Selby Plummer to be indicative of 'some tubercular mischief'. If this is true, then the saint had a form of tuberculosis that spread throughout his body, and was not just restricted to his lungs.

Selby Plummer had an opportunity to make a careful examination of Cuthbert's remains when the grave was opened in 1899. He found no evidence on the body to support his tubercular theory, but then the body he saw was very old, and may not have been Cuthbert's at all. The Roman Catholics of the north-east have long maintained that another body was substituted for Cuthbert's at the Reformation.

Today we tend to associate tuberculosis with overcrowded Victorian slums, and heroines in romantic nineteenth-century operas, but this disease has accompanied mankind through history, from very ancient times.

Whether or not it was tuberculosis, Cuthbert seems to have had some kind of chronic or intermittent medical problem, and Bede is quick to point out his similarity in this regard to St Paul, who had a mysterious condition that troubled him 'like a thorn in the flesh' for much of his life.

Although evidence of chronic disease seems to have been missing, the examinations of Cuthbert's skull in 1827 and 1899 determined that, though the skull itself was rather small, the nose and chin would have been large and impressive in life, and that Cuthbert was lucky enough to have some teeth still in his head when he died, despite being quite an old man at death, by Anglo-Saxon standards.

It was during the 1827 examination that the famous pectoral cross was discovered. This is one of the great treasures of Durham Cathedral, is used as a logo or symbol by many local organisations, and now features on the new County Durham flag.

As well as what we might call his excessively ascetic way of life, another characteristic of Cuthbert that won't be admired by many modern readers is his sectarian prejudice. Although, on his death-bed, he counsels Abbot Herefrid to show hospitality to Christians, he excludes those who are not Catholic, and who therefore celebrate Easter at the 'wrong' time. This, and other episodes in Bede's book, are reminders of the conflict between the Catholic and Celtic forms of Christianity in the Britain of Cuthbert's day.

Although some aspects of Cuthbert's life may strike modern readers as strange, it is clear that, in his book, Bede is trying to foreground the parts of his character that religious readers of his own time would have found most admirable. Part of this process involves pushing other aspects out to the background; and we have to read between the lines to pick up the clues that Bede has left us.

A superficial reading of Bede's book leaves the impression that Cuthbert was a humble shepherd who joined a monastery and rose to the office of bishop by merit alone. This is almost certainly wrong. When Cuthbert first appears at Boisil's monastery at Melrose, he is riding a horse and carrying a spear. In Anglo-Saxon Britain, these were both signs of wealth and high status.

Another factor that seems to indicate Cuthbert's blue-blooded background is the fact that he had a nurse when he was a child. Bede doesn't name this lady, though he does mention her. The author of the slightly earlier *Anonymous Life of Cuthbert* calls her Kenswith, and says that she looked after him from the age of eight, until he was a man. Aristocratic Anglo-Saxons would often farm out their children to foster-mothers in this way, much as some parents from the middle and upper classes in England still banish their children to so-called public schools, where many live as boarders. The author of the anonymous life tells us that Kenswith was a widow and a nun. Both Bede and the anonymous monk agree that Cuthbert called her 'Mother'.

It is interesting to note that, according to Bede, it was at the age of eight that Cuthbert began to take life more seriously, and felt the beginnings of his religious vocation. The immediate cause of this is supposed to have been a little child who acted as a mouthpiece for God, and rebuked Cuthbert for his foolish behaviour. But it may be that, at this time, the influence of the pious Kenswith began to have its effect.

Another proof of Cuthbert's high birth is the fact that, when he is crippled by a tumour in his leg, there are servants to carry him outside, to sit in the sun.

17

Many of the bishops, abbots and abbesses with whom Cuthbert had dealings are also known to have been of aristocratic birth: sometimes Bede reminds us of this, and suggests that their noble blood sits well with the nobility of their Christian calling. The fact that Cuthbert was able to converse as an equal with these people suggests that he came from the same class. Against this background, it would seem that Cuthbert's stint as a shepherd was part of some scheme of manhood-training for aristocratic boys.

The missionaries who converted the Anglo-Saxons to Christianity usually started with the highest ranks, thinking, perhaps, that once the local monarch converted, his subjects would follow suit. The interesting episode where the young Cuthbert's prayers save some monks from drowning may shed light on the patchy effect of this missionary strategy. Standing on the bank of the river, Cuthbert finds himself among commoners who curse the monks, hope they will drown, and complain about their newfangled religion, which nobody can understand.

This episode is not the only one where the spiritual backsliding of the people is shown. When the plague returns to Northumbria, some of the people go back to their old pagan superstitions, 'using chants and amulets, and other mysteries of witchcraft'. This tendency for people, especially in remote areas, to revert to pagan practices seems to be one reason why Cuthbert as a bishop is assiduous in visiting these places, some of which don't even have a church, or a building big enough to hold a meeting.

A careful reading of Bede's *Prose Life of St Cuthbert* brings to light more than just the class structure of Anglo-Saxon society, and the effect that that hierarchy had on the spiritual lives of the people. Bede's book also offers a picture of other aspects of life in this time and place.

The men and women in Bede's narrative have a strong tendency to cry copious tears, and to embrace each other in a highly emotional manner. To modern English readers, this might come over as a sign of weakness or mental imbalance, but we must remember that Bede was writing before the days of the 'stiff upper lip', when emotional restraint became *de rigeur*, especially for English men. Even if he hadn't suffered from tuberculosis, Cuthbert may have cried more freely that Britishers today.

A lot of the action of the book takes place in the open air. In Anglo-Saxon times, it would often be lighter, warmer, more private, and also healthier outside than it would be in a dark, smoky hall, or a hut made of wattle and daub.

It is clear from the book that travel was slow, dangerous and difficult in those days, yet Cuthbert and his spiritual associates would travel long distances by river, sea or land. Their journeys would often take them into wildernesses where food and shelter would be hard to find.

A more attractive aspect of travel in this period seems to be that the people regarded hospitality very highly, and would try hard to make even unexpected guests welcome, sharing whatever food, drink and accommodation they had. Cuthbert applies the rules of hospitality even to animals, sharing an early form of sandwich with his horse, and sharing a fish with an eagle. The animal kingdom reciprocates in the episode where the sea-otters warm and dry Cuthbert's feet – earlier in Bede's book, we read about how Cuthbert tried to warm and dry the feet of a guest, who turned out to be an angel.

Travel by sea, river and land was of course the way that diseases like the bubonic plague could spread in those days, and in Bede's narrative plague is just one of a number of diseases for which the doctors of the time have no answer. One reason why Bede features so many miraculous cures in his book is perhaps because illness was terrifying and mysterious to these people. Both physical and mental diseases appear in Bede's pages, and Bede shows little doubt that he blames mental illness on possession by demons. This is entirely in line with Christian medical opinion in the Middle Ages, and the idea is sanctioned by the Gospels, where Jesus casts out demons and thus cures people we would now think of as mentally ill.

When their lives and their sanity were not being threatened by disease or famine, the Anglo-Saxons of Bede's time could still find their lives shortened by war, as happens to King Ecgfrid 'and his entire bodyguard' in the course of Bede's narrative. This was liable to happen, as the Britain of this time was divided into many different petty kingdoms, which were often at war with each other.

The culture of the Anglo-Saxon aristocracy was warlike in nature, and of course where boys are bred up to be warriors, they are likely to expect war when they are men. We should not forget that the Anglo-Saxon period left us the poem *Beowulf* as well as the writings of Bede.

We might assume that by entering a monastery, Cuthbert was avoiding conflict, but Bede is convinced that Cuthbert fought many hard spiritual battles, 'armed with the helmet of salvation, the shield of faith, and the sword of the Spirit'.

The many miracles recounted in Bede's book may put off some modern readers, who will naturally ask, can these stories be true, and did Bede himself believe in them?

The chances are that if Bede were summoned back from the dead and asked if the stories in his book were true, he would have trouble understanding the question, even if it were put to him in Medieval Latin, or Old English. Bede was not an ideal historian in the modern sense – he wasn't interested just in facts, and he seems to have had no interest in producing a frank, warts-and-all portrait of Cuthbert.

Bede had an agenda – he wanted to show the power of the Christian God as it manifested itself through a saint. Bede also wanted to show that an English saint could be just as miraculous as, say, St Antony of Egypt; that the age of miracles had not passed, and that British history was just as worthy a subject for a chronicler as, for instance, the history of Rome.

He was also keen to promote the Latin or Roman Catholic form of Christianity, which in Cuthbert's time still existed alongside the distinctive Celtic variety.

Bede doesn't explicitly mention the conflict between the Celtic and Catholic ways in his *Prose Life of St Cuthbert*, but when we read that Cuthbert didn't want to be buried on land ruled by 'schismatics', that he worked hard to convert some of the Lindisfarne monks from their old ways, and that there was serious trouble in the diocese after his death, we can feel some of this background coming through.

The conflict, known as the Paschal Controversy because it concerned the correct calculation of the date of Easter, is treated at length in Bede's *Ecclesiastical History*. The battle was particularly relevant to the English, or Anglo-Saxons, of Cuthbert's time because they had been pagans when they first came to Britain, and had been converted to Christianity from two directions, by the Irish from the north-west, and by Rome from the south-east.

By the seventh century it was felt that these two systems couldn't coexist in Northumbria, and in 664 a historic synod at Whitby decided in favour of the Roman way.

The purpose of the following version of Bede's

Prose Life of St Cuthbert is to provide a readable, accurate and complete version of the book, which was originally written in the Latin of the clerics of eighth century Northumbria.

I have worked from the foundation of the classic English translation published by Joseph Stevenson in 1887, but I have also referred to translations by J.F. Webb and Bertram Colgrave. I have sometimes referred to the Latin text printed in Colgrave's edition, which contains both Bede's book and another life of Cuthbert, by an anonymous monk of Lindisfarne.

As Colgrave points out, Bede's treatment is sometimes a little long-winded: where he has used repetitions, clarifications, rhetorical flourishes and pious epithets that add little to the story, I have carefully and respectfully pruned these back.

Where Bede calls Cuthbert 'the man of God,' I have sometimes substituted 'Cuthbert' or 'the saint', and where the word 'he' or 'she' appears, and it seems unclear to whom Bede is referring, I have inserted the most likely name.

In trying to make the text modern, I haven't always been able to find suitable modern terms to replace words Stevenson renders as, for instance, 'contrition'. Where this seems to have worked, I have replaced, for instance, 'virtue' with 'goodness', and 'schismatics' with the phrase 'people who bring disunity to the church'. For the sake of clarity, I have sometimes substituted the word 'monks' for 'brothers'. In this and many other things I have followed the examples of the creators of modern English versions of the Scriptures, such as J.B. Phillips, K.N. Taylor and E.H. Peterson. Readers wanting a more literal translation (rather than a careful paraphrase) should get hold of those by Stevenson, Colgrave or J.F. Webb (see bibliography).

Beyond the simple replacement of words and phrases, I have often felt it necessary to break up Bede and Stevenson's long, grammatically complex sentences into smaller, simpler units. I have taken a similar approach to paragraphs.

I have used Bede's chapter-numbers throughout, but I have removed his chapter-headings. These, and some of Bede's repetitions, indicate that the chapters of his book were intended to be studied or read aloud individually, not just read together as a continuous narrative. I have introduced the division of the book, and of Cuthbert's life, into sections numbered I-V.

A few notes have been added using asterisks, which lead to the end of the relevant chapter-section as used by Bede. Biblical quotations are from the King James Version, followed by Bible locations in square brackets where necessary.

SW, Durham, January 2014

Bede's Preface

To the holy and blessed Bishop Edfrid, and all the monks who serve Christ on the island of Lindisfarne, Bede, your faithful colleague, sends greetings.

You asked me, my dear brothers, to write the usual preface to my book about the blessed St Cuthbert, and so, to please you and to show my obedience, I have done so. I would like to use this preface to assure those who know about the saint, and also those who know nothing about him, that I have not written down anything that has not been thoroughly researched, and also checked by surviving witnesses of the events.

In fact, I wrote nothing until I had investigated everything very carefully, for instance by questioning people who had known Cuthbert. Occasionally I mention the names of these witnesses, to assure readers that what I have written is true.

After I had completed the first draft of my little work, I kept it back in manuscript, and showed it frequently to our most reverend brother Herefrid, the priest, when he came here. I also showed it to several other people, who had lived for a long time with the man of God, and knew the details of his life. I did this so that they could read it, and carefully correct or delete what they thought should be deleted or corrected.

I have carefully made some of the changes they suggested, as seemed good to me. And thus all doubts having been completely removed, I have dared to commit the result of this careful research, written in simple language, to these few sheets of parchment.

When I sent you what I had written, dear brother, you were kind enough to make your own suggestions for changes. At that time my little work was read out to the elders and the more well-read members of your congregation. After every part had been carefully examined, it was found unnecessary to change a single word. Everything that had been written was pronounced worthy, by common consent, to be read with confidence.

It was also judged suitable to be copied by anyone whose devotion prompted them to do so. In the course of this investigation and discussion, you revealed, when I was there, that there were many other events relating to the life and miracles of Cuthbert, of no less importance than those which I had recorded, which were worthy of being preserved. But by that time it seemed wrong to add new material to a work that had already been finished and considered.

It seems right to me that I should ask your holy community for their prayers of intercession, since I have done my duty and followed your commands. I hope that when you re-read this little book you will remember your holy father, aspire to the heavenly kingdom, and not forget to pray for forgiveness for my poor self. Pray that I may now desire, with a pure mind, 'to see the goodness of the Lord in the land of the living.' [Psalm 27]

I also ask that when I am dead, you will pray for the soul of myself, your friend and servant. Please offer masses for me, and write my name in the list of members of your holy community. Remember, most holy prelate, that you have already promised that this will be done; and to prove it, you have already commanded Gudfrid, the sacristan, to write my name in the register of your holy congregation.

Let me also tell you, my holy brother, that I have recently written a shorter life of Cuthbert in heroic verse: this was done at the request of some of the monks here.

You can get a copy of this poem from me: in the preface I promised to write a longer account of his life and miracles. This promise I have now carried out as quickly as I could in the present little work, to the best of the abilities granted to me by God.

Praying, therefore, for you, my most beloved brothers and masters, that the Almighty Lord will keep you safe in your present blessed state.

Amen.

I. Boyhood of a Saint

1. I would like to make the beginning of this account of the life of the blessed Cuthbert holy, by quoting the words of the prophet Jeremiah. When he is praising the anchorite's perfection, he says: 'It is good that a man should both hope and quietly wait for the salvation of the Lord. It is good for a man that he bear the yoke in his youth. He sitteth alone and keepeth silence, because he hath borne it upon him.' [Lamentations 3: 26-8]

In this way, Cuthbert the man of God bowed his neck to the monastic yoke from early youth. He was so inflamed with the sweetness of the holy anchorite's life, that whenever possible, he eagerly grasped at it. He rejoiced 'to sit alone and keep silent' for long periods, away from all human contact, in the sweetness of divine contemplation. In this way, heavenly grace steadily urged him on into the way of truth: this was so that his own grace might increase more and more as he grew older, even from the first years of his boyhood.

Until his eighth year (which is the first year when an infant becomes a boy) he gave his mind entirely to the usual games and silliness of children, so that he might be said to be a living testimony of what is recorded in the book of Samuel: 'Now

Cuthbert did not yet know the Lord, neither was the word of the Lord yet revealed unto him.' [adapted from 1 Samuel 3:7]

So he deserves more praise, because when he was older he came to 'know the Lord' perfectly, and to hear the Word of the Lord with the opened ears of the heart.

But at this time, as I have said, Cuthbert took great pleasure in jokes and childish games. As was in keeping with his age, he loved to be in the company of other boys, and to join with them in all their sports.

As he was active and witty by nature, he was usually the champion in all such games; so that sometimes when the rest were tired out, he would ask, as a joyous victor, if there were any that could still contend with him?

Whether they practised leaping or running or wrestling, or any other sport which required agility, he boasted that he outdid all his equals in age, and sometimes even older boys. For when he was a child he spoke as a child, he understood as a child; but when he became a man, he entirely put away the things of a child. [paraphrase of 1 Corinthians 13:11]

But divine providence, through a handy mouthpiece, soon tried to restrain the buoyancy of this childish spirit. Bishop Trumwine of blessed memory confirmed that Cuthbert had himself told him how this happened.

'One day,' he said, 'a number of boys, of whom

he was one, were engaged as usual in wrestling in a meadow; and as many of them, with the typical thoughtlessness of boyhood, were twisting their limbs into various unnatural shapes, suddenly one of these children, who seemed to be about three years old, ran up to Cuthbert. With the gravity of old age, he began to beg him not to join in with these silly sports, but to think and behave more seriously.

'Cuthbert paid no attention to these words, and the little fellow who had spoken them threw himself to the ground, and, with tears running down his cheeks, showed signs of great grief. Some ran to comfort him, but he still carried on weeping. Then they asked him what had happened to him to make him cry. As Cuthbert himself was comforting him, he said: "Why do you behave like this, against nature and your own rank, Cuthbert, most holy prelate and priest? It doesn't suit you to play among children, when the Lord has picked you out to be a teacher of goodness, even to people who are older than you!"

'When young Cuthbert, who was at heart a good boy, heard these words, he paid close attention to them, and kindly and affectionately soothed the weeping child: and he immediately decided to give up his silly sports. Returning home, he began to be more serious and manly in his behaviour. The Holy Spirit Himself taught him, in his inmost heart, the message the little boy had delivered.

'Nobody should be surprised that the Lord should restrain the gaiety of the boy with the words of a child: once it pleased Him to silence the madness of a prophet by putting the words of reason into the mouth of an animal.* In His praise it has been truly said: 'Out of the mouth of babes and sucklings thou hast perfected praise.' [Matthew 21:16]

*This is the story of Balaam and the ass (Numbers 22: 21-38)

2. It is written that 'unto every one that hath shall be given, and he shall have abundance.' [Matthew 25:29] That is to say, a great deal more purpose and love of goodness will be given to a man who already has a sense of purpose, and a love of goodness. So from the time that Cuthbert, the servant of the Lord, took to heart the lesson he had heard from the little boy, he was comforted by the vision and the voice of an angel.

On one occasion he had a sudden pain in his knee, and the knee began to swell into a foul-smelling tumour. This made the nerves of his leg contract, and he was forced to keep one foot off the ground, and limp from place to place. Eventually the problem got so bad that he was no longer able to walk at all.

One day, when he had been carried out of doors by his servants, and was lying down in the open air, he suddenly saw in the distance a noble-looking rider, clothed in white, sitting on a beautiful horse.

As he came up, the rider politely saluted

Cuthbert, and asked him if he could help him. Cuthbert said, 'I wish I could stand up and help *you*, but, for my sins, I have been crippled and made a prisoner by this disease. I have been suffering from this swollen knee for a long time, and no doctor can heal me.'

At that, the stranger leaped from his horse and carefully examined the diseased knee. Then he said, 'You should boil some wheat-flour in milk, and cover the tumour with the poultice, while it's still warm. That will heal you.' Saying this, the horseman mounted and rode off. Cuthbert, following his instructions, was healed in a few days. He realised that it was an angel who had given him this advice; an angel sent by Him who once promised to send the archangel Raphael to restore sight to Tobias. [in the Book of Tobit, considered apocryphal by e.g. the Church of England]

If it seems incredible to anyone that an angel would appear on horseback, let him read the history of the Maccabees, where it says that angels came on horseback to defend Judas Maccabeus and the temple of God.

3. From this time on, this devout servant of the Lord (as he later told his friends) was often rescued from his difficulties by angels, once he had prayed to the Lord. Yes, even when he prayed for other people who were in danger, his prayers were heard by Him Who always hears the 'poor that call on Him, and delivers them out of all their troubles.' [paraphrase

of part of Psalm 34]

Now there is a monastery not far from the mouth of the river Tyne, towards the south. This was then a community of men, but now it has changed, as all things change in this world, into a thriving community of nuns who serve Christ.

Those servants of Christ were transporting wood from far away on rafts on the river (this wood was to be used by the monks). When the monks on the rafts arrived opposite the monastery, they tried to get to the shore, but a stormy wind blew up from the west. This caught the rafts, and they began to drift toward the mouth of the river.

Their brother monks saw this from the monastery, and launched some boats onto the river to rescue the men on the rafts. But, overpowered by the current and a strong wind, they couldn't manage a rescue. Giving up on human aid, they called on divine aid. They came out of the monastery as the rafts were drifting out to sea. Gathering together on the nearest piece of dry land, they bent their knees and prayed to the Lord for those they saw drifting, so it seemed, to their deaths.

The earnest prayers of the brothers were unanswered, and for this reason – so that divine providence could show the power of Cuthbert's prayers.

On the opposite bank of the river, where Cuthbert himself stood, there was a large crowd of the common people. As the monks looked on sadly, they saw the rafts driven out to sea, till they looked like five little birds floating on the waves. Then the people began to jeer at the monks and their way of life, as if people who ignored the ways of mortals, and had introduced a strange new way of life, deserved to suffer such a disaster.

Cuthbert, however, stopped the jeers of the mockers, saying, 'What are you doing, brothers, speaking evil against those you see being hurried away toward death? Wouldn't it be better to pray to the Lord for their safety, rather than laugh at their peril?' But chafing against him, with brutish minds and tongues, they replied, 'Let no one pray for them; may God have pity on none of them! They have taken away our old religion, and no one knows how to follow the new religion!'

On hearing this answer, Cuthbert bent his knees in prayer to the Lord, and bowed his head to the ground. Soon the strong winds turned around, and brought the rafts back to the beach in safety. The men who had tried to steer them were very happy, and the rafts landed very near the monastery.

On seeing this, the crowd of peasants blushed in embarrassment because of their lack of faith, and declared that they believed in the venerable Cuthbert. From then on they kept on declaring it, as I was told by a certain most respected brother of our monastery, from whom I learned this story. He told me he had heard it, in the presence of many others, from one of those very peasants, a man of great simplicity, who could never have made up something like that.

4. The grace of Christ, which rules the lives of the faithful, decided that His servant should live a more disciplined life, and thus win the glory of a greater reward.

At this time, Cuthbert was keeping watch over flocks of sheep on some remote mountains. One night he was staying awake, praying through the night, with his companions sleeping beside him. Suddenly he saw a light streaming down from heaven, breaking through the darkness. In the light were choirs of angels coming down to earth, and after taking away a soul that was full of light, they returned to their heavenly country.

Cuthbert, who was loved by God, was touched by this vision, and decided to use all his energies to achieve grace like that, and come to know such glorious beings in everlasting life and happiness.

So Cuthbert immediately gave praise and thanksgiving to God, and with brotherly encouragement woke up his companions so that they too could praise the Lord.

'Alas!,' he said; 'because we're so sleepy and drowsy, we can't see the light of the servants of Christ, who never sleep. While I was awake and praying, I saw the wonderful works of God. I saw the gate of heaven opened, and the spirit of some saint carried up by a crowd of angels. While we lie here in darkness, that saint can see the glory of the heavenly mansion, and Christ its King.

'Really, I think that the person I saw being

carried away into the light, with choirs of angels leading him to heaven, must have been a holy bishop, or some other excellent, faithful man.'

By saying this, Cuthbert, the man of God, inspired the hearts of the other shepherds to worship and praise God. When morning came, they learned that Aidan, the bishop of the church of Lindisfarne, a man of great goodness, had died at the very time Cuthbert had seen him being carried up to heaven. Cuthbert returned the sheep he had been watching to their owners, and decided to enter a monastery.

5. His mind was now completely serious, and he was ready for a more structured way of life. Heavenly grace helped him to be decisive about this, and it showed him that people who look for the kingdom of God and His goodness will always find food to eat.

One day at about nine o'clock in the morning*, Cuthbert was travelling alone. He turned aside into a farm, which he had spotted from a long way off. At the farm, he entered the house of a devout woman, hoping to rest for a little while, caring more about getting food for his horse than for himself, as it was the beginning of winter. The woman of the house welcomed him kindly, and begged him to allow her to prepare a meal. But the man of God refused, saying, 'I mustn't eat yet, because this is a fast day.' It was a Friday, when most faithful people go without food until as late as three o'clock in the afternoon, out of respect for the crucifixion of Jesus.

The woman, keen to be hospitable, carried on pressing him. 'Remember,' she said, 'that on your journey you'll find no village or other settlement. You still have a long way to go, and you can't possibly arrive before sunset. I beg you to take some food before setting out, or you'll be forced to fast all day, or perhaps even till tomorrow.' But Cuthbert's love of religion held out against her, and he spent the rest of the day fasting, until the evening.

He realised, as evening was coming on, that he could not finish his journey that day, and that there was no house nearby where he could take shelter for the night. But he suddenly noticed some shepherds' huts. These had been roughly put together in summer, and now stood deserted and in ruins. He entered one of these, hoping to pass the night inside. He tied his horse to the wall and gave him a bundle of hay to eat (the wind had pulled this hay off the roof).

He himself spent the time in prayer, but as he was singing a psalm he noticed his horse raising his head, and pulling at the inside of the thatching of the hut. As he pulled down the straw, a folded napkin fell out.

When he had finished his prayer, Cuthbert looked inside the napkin and found half of a loaf of bread, still warm, and a piece of meat, enough to make a meal for himself. Praising this heavenly gift, he said 'I give thanks to God, Who has provided a supper for me. I was fasting for Him, but He has fed me and my companion, the horse.' Then he divided the piece of bread he had found, and gave one half of it to his horse, saving the rest for himself.

From that day on he became more ready to go without food, since he understood that there would always be food ready for him in the wilderness, prepared by Him who fed old Elijah the hermit. Elijah also had no one to serve food to him, but he was fed by birds. [1 Kings 17] This shows that: 'the eye of the Lord is upon them that fear him, upon them that hope in his mercy; to deliver their soul from death, and to keep them alive in famine.' [from Psalm 33]

I heard this story from a devout priest of our monastery, which is at the mouth of the river Wear. This man, called Inguald, looks forward with a pure heart to heavenly things rather than to earthly things, since he has now reached a good old age. Ingauld also told me that he heard this story from Cuthbert himself, after he was a bishop.

* Bede says 'at the third hour'. In Anglo-Saxon times, the hours were often counted from about six in the morning, which was called 'prime'. I have converted the Anglo-Saxon times in Bede's text into their modern equivalents.

II. Cuthbert as a Monk

6. Meanwhile this venerable servant of the Lord, having given up all earthly concerns, was eager to put himself under monastic discipline as soon as possible. He felt that he had been summoned, by the heavenly vision he had seen, to seek the joys of everlasting blessedness; been invited to eat food from heaven, and to suffer hunger and thirst in this world for the Lord.

Although he knew that there were many holy men at the church on Lindisfarne, who could all teach him, the fame and goodness of Boisil, a monk and priest, made him decide to go to Melrose* instead.

When he arrived there, he leaped from his horse and was about to enter the church to pray. He gave his horse to an attendant, as well as the spear which he held in his hand (as he was not yet dressed as a monk). Then Boisil himself, who was standing at the gate of the monastery, saw him for the first time. Sensing Cuthbert's future greatness, Boisil said, 'Behold, a servant of God!' This was like Jesus, Who, when he first saw Nathaniel, said 'Behold, an Israelite indeed, in whom there is no guile.' [John 1:47]

Sigfrid, a devout priest, and a trusty servant of

the Lord, used to assure us that this was true: he was standing by, with some other people, when Boisil said this. At that time, he was a young man in the same monastery, and he was learning the first lessons of the monastic life. He is still alive, a perfect monk, and he lives in our monastery at Jarrow. As he breathes his last breaths here, this Sigfrid thirsts after a joyful entrance into another life.

Boisil didn't say any more, but greeted Cuthbert kindly as he came to him. When Cuthbert had explained that he wanted to live in a monastery rather than in the world, Boisil stayed with him, as he was the prior of that monastery.

A few days afterwards, the blessed Eata arrived. He was then a priest, and the abbot of Melrose: later he became the abbot of Lindisfarne, and bishop of the church of Lindisfarne. Boisil spoke to Eata about Cuthbert, telling him he was ready for the monastic life. Then the prior got permission from the abbot to give Cuthbert the tonsure, and allow him to mix with the rest of the brothers.

After he entered the monastery, Cuthbert immediately worked hard to follow the rule of the place with as much enthusiasm as the rest of the community. In fact he was more hard-working than all the others, in reading, working with his hands, staying awake, and praying. Like Samson, who was a Nazarite, and the strongest of men, Cuthbert carefully avoided anything that could get him drunk. And he didn't want to overdo the fasting, in case he became unfit for work. He had a strong, robust body, and could do any kind of work he tried.

* Old Melrose, some two miles from the present abbey.

7. Some years later King Alchfrid, for the sake of his soul, gave to an abbot called Eata a place called Ripon, to build a monastery. Eata took some monks along with him, including Cuthbert, and he founded the monastery.

In the new monastery, Eata brought in the same regular discipline he had introduced at Melrose. Here Cuthbert, the servant of the Lord, was given the job of guest master. At this time, it is said that he acted as host to an angel of the Lord, which proved how devoted he was to God.

Early one morning, he left the inner buildings of the monastery and went out to the guest-chamber. He found a young man sitting there, and, thinking that he was mortal, he immediately welcomed him with his usual kindness. He gave him water to wash his hands, and he himself washed his feet. He wiped the man's feet with a towel, then placed them against his chest to warm them, humbly rubbing them with his hands. He asked the man to remain until nine o'clock, when he would get some food. He warned him that if he continued on his journey with an empty stomach, he would suffer from hunger as well as the winter's cold.

Cuthbert thought the stranger had been worn out

by a night-journey as well as by the snowy blasts, and that he had come there at dawn to have a rest. The man said that he could not rest: he said that he had to leave soon, because he still had a long way to go. But Cuthbert kept on asking him to stay, and at last, using the Divine Name, he forced him to remain. Immediately after the prayers of the hour of terce* were finished, and breakfast-time was approaching, he laid the table and offered him food, saying, 'I beg you, brother, feed yourself until I come back with some fresh bread: I expect the new bread will be ready by now.'

When he returned, he didn't find the guest he had left at the table. Looking outside for his footprints, he saw none, although a recent fall of snow had covered the ground. Puzzled, the man of God replaced the table in the inner apartment. As he went in there, he sensed a marvellously pleasant smell. On looking round to see where the sweet smell came from, he saw lying beside him three warm loaves of amazing whiteness and beauty.

Trembling, he said to himself, 'I think I have just played host to an angel of God, who came to feed rather than to be fed. He has brought loaves such as this earth cannot produce; they are whiter that lilies, smell better than roses, and taste better than honey. It is clear, then, that they are not from this earth, but have been brought from the paradise of Eden. It is no marvel that someone who eats the bread of eternal life in heaven should refuse to eat earthly food.'

From that time on, the man of God was more humble, because he had witnessed such a mighty miracle, and he put even more effort into his good works. As he did more good, his grace also increased. From that time on, he was very often allowed to see and talk with angels, and when he was hungry, he fed on food prepared for him by a special gift of the Lord.

As Cuthbert was friendly and had pleasant manners, he would often re-tell the deeds of the fathers who came before him, to anyone who was with him, as an example for them to imitate. He also used to humbly mix in something about the spiritual gifts which heaven had given to him. He sometimes did this openly, but he usually took care to do it under a veil, as if it had happened to some other person. Nevertheless, the people who heard him understood that he was speaking about himself. In this he was like the great prophet of the Gentiles**, who sometimes made an open display of his own gifts, and at other times spoke as if he were talking about another person; for instance when he said, 'I knew a man in Christ above fourteen years ago...such an one caught up to the third heaven.' [2 Corinthians 12:2]

*Nine o'clock in the morning.
** St Paul.

8. Meanwhile, since the whole world is fragile, and as unsteady as the sea when a sudden storm blows up, Abbot Eata, with Cuthbert, and the rest of the monks he had brought with him, were driven home, and the site of the monastery which he had founded was given to other monks. But Cuthbert, that memorable soldier of Christ, did not change his mind with his change of location, and he didn't turn his back on his decision to wage heavenly warfare. With as much care as he had always used, he gave close attention to the words and example of the blessed Boisil.

At this time, as Herefrid says, Cuthbert went down with the plague. (Herefrid was his friend and priest, and had once been abbot of the monastery of Lindisfarne.)

Many were dying of the plague at that time, throughout the length and breadth of Britain. The monks were awake all night, praying for Cuthbert's recovery, because they all thought that his life was necessary to them, because he was such a holy man. Next morning, when some of the monks told him they had done this, he said, 'Why am I still lying here? God will not ignore the prayers of so many of His devout servants. Give me my staff and stockings.'

He got up immediately, and began trying to walk, leaning on his staff. His strength increased every day, and he was soon completely healthy, but although the tumour which appeared on his thigh stopped swelling, it gradually sank beneath the surface of his skin, and settled in his bowels. He continued to feel a little pain inside his body for most of the rest of his life, so that, like the apostle, his power was 'made perfect in weakness.' [2 Corinthians 12:9]

When Boisil, the servant of the Lord, saw Cuthbert on his feet once more, he said, 'You see, brother, that you are now freed from the pain that afflicted you, and I say to you, that you will not suffer any more illness now, nor will you die at this time. All the same I warn you, since death is now ready for me, to learn something from me, as long as I am able to teach you. I have not more than seven days left, in which I shall have a healthy body, and strength of tongue to teach.'

Without doubting the truth of his master's words, Cuthbert replied: 'What should I read, which I can get through in one week?'

'John the Evangelist,' Boisil replied. 'I have a copy, divided into seven gatherings, one of which, with the Lord's help, we can read each day, and as far as is necessary, discuss it.'

So they did as they had agreed. They got through this reading quickly, as it didn't deal with deep questions, but only with the simplicity of the faith that works through love. They completed the reading in seven days, and then Boisil, who had been attacked by the plague, came to his last day. After this, he entered into the joys of everlasting light.

It is said that during these seven days he told

Cuthbert everything that was going to happen to him in the future: as I said before, Boisil was a very holy man, and he had the gift of prophecy. He also predicted that the strength of the plague which was then raging would continue for three years, before it infected abbot Eata, his son. He also revealed that Eata would be killed by it; but he added that the abbot would not die of plague as such, but of dysentery. All this happened as he predicted.

He also informed Cuthbert that he would become a bishop. But Cuthbert, when he later withdrew from the world and became an anchorite, would not tell anyone that Boisil had predicted this. He had a habit of saying, with much sorrow, to the monks who occasionally visited him, 'That if it were possible that I could hide myself in a tiny cave, on a cliff where the waves of the swelling ocean would surround me, and shut me out from the sight of all men, even then I wouldn't think of myself as free from the snares of this world. In my cave, I would be afraid that greed would tempt me to leave my cave, or give me some other reason to leave it.'

9. After the death of Boisil, the priest so loved by God, Cuthbert became prior of Melrose. He did that job for several years, with a great deal of saintly, spiritual zeal. He gave the whole community not only his advice on the spiritual life, but also his example of how to live as a monk. He was also enthusiastic about converting all the people for miles around from their former foolish life, and leading them to the love of heavenly joys. At that time,

many of them were too wicked to live like proper Christians.

At the time of the plague, some of the local people even neglected their Christian faith, and tried pagan medicines. They tried to halt the progress of the plague (which had been sent by God their Maker) by using chants and amulets, and other mysteries of witchcraft. To correct these errors, Cuthbert frequently went out from the monastery, sometimes on horseback, but usually on foot, and preached the way of truth to those who had gone wrong, as Boisil had done in his day.

In those days, when a cleric or priest came into a village, it was the custom of the English people for all the villagers to flock together to hear the Word. They would willingly listen to what was said, and would follow up what they had heard with good works. Cuthbert's skill in teaching was so great, his power of loving persuasion was so vast, and the light of his angelic face was so striking, that no one dared to hide the hidden secrets of his heart. Everybody openly confessed what they had done wrong, knowing that none of these sins were concealed from Cuthbert. And everyone worked to wipe away the sins they had confessed, as Cuthbert commanded, with the fruits of penance.

Cuthbert also used to seek out, and preach in, remote villages, located far from the world, in wild, scary mountain places. These places were so poor and remote that they seldom saw any kind of teacher. Giving himself up to this work with a good will, Cuthbert worked on these remote districts and people with so much learning and enthusiasm, that he often didn't return home to his monastery for an entire week, sometimes for two or three, and occasionally for even a full month. During this time he remained in the mountains, and called the inhabitants back to the things of heaven, by the word of his preaching as well as by the example of his goodness.

10. As this holy man was steadily becoming more virtuous, and performing more miracles, the news of his life was spreading everywhere. At this time a holy nun and mother-superior of Christ's handmaidens, called Ebba, was ruling a convent at a place called Coldingham.

This abbess was as noble in religion as she was by birth, as everyone agreed, as she was a sister of King Oswiu. She sent to the man of God, begging him to come and bless herself and her nuns with his teaching. Cuthbert could not refuse what God's handmaid had begged for.

So he went to Coldingham, stayed there for some days, and explained the way of justice to everyone. He not only preached this, but also practised it.

While the rest of the community was asleep, it was his habit to go out alone and spend most of the night in prayer and vigils. He didn't return home till the hour of the common service was near. One night, one of the monks of the monastery, seeing him go out in silence, followed him to find out where he was going, and why.

Cuthbert, followed by the spy, went straight to the sea- shore below the monastery. Wading out into the water till the waves reached to his neck, he spent the darkness of the night saying prayers, accompanied by the sound of the waves. Near dawn, he went up the beach, and finished his prayer on bended knees.

As he was doing this, two otters, who had come out of the sea and were stretched out on the sand in front of Cuthbert, began to warm his feet with their breath. They also wiped them dry with their fur. As soon as they had finished, Cuthbert gave them his blessing, and dismissed them back to the sea, while he himself returned to the house to recite the morning psalms with the monks.

Meanwhile the monk who had been watching him from his hiding-place, was filled with so much fear, that he could only get home with great difficulty, and with tottering steps. Early in the morning he came to Cuthbert, and throwing himself on the ground in front of him, begged pardon with tears in his eyes for his foolish exploit (he had never doubted that Cuthbert knew what he had done during the night, and how much he had suffered).

Cuthbert asked him, 'What is the matter, brother; what have you done? Have you tried to spy out why I go out at night? I forgive you, but on one condition: that you promise not to tell anybody about what you saw, until I am dead.' In this way, Cuthbert followed the example of Him, Who, when

He had shown the glory of His majesty to His disciples on the Mount, said, 'Tell the vision to no man, until the Son of Man be risen again from the dead.' [Matthew 17:9]

When the monk had promised this, Cuthbert gave him his blessing, wiping away his sin as well as the guilt he felt. The monk, keeping his promise, hid the miracle he had seen in the silence of his heart as long as Cuthbert lived; though he told the story to many people after the saint's death.

11. Meanwhile the man of God began to become a powerful prophet, predicting future things, and giving accurate accounts of far-away events as if he were present at them. On one occasion, as he set out from his monastery on some necessary business, he boarded a ship that was going to Niduari, in the land of the Picts.* He was accompanied by two monks, one of whom, who later became a priest, told everybody about the miracle Cuthbert performed at that time.

They had arrived after Christmas Day, expecting a speedy return, because the waves seemed to be smiling at them, and the winds were favourable. Because of this, they had taken no food with them. Unfortunately, things didn't go as well as they had expected. Scarcely had they reached the land, when a wild storm blew up, which prevented them from sailing home. For several days they suffered cold and hunger. Nevertheless the man of God would not spend even this time in sluggish idleness, or give himself up to lazy sleep. Instead, he took care to continue praying all night.

Now, the most holy day of our Lord's Epiphany was at hand, so Cuthbert spoke encouragingly to his companions, as he was always pleasant and affable.

'Why should we become drowsy and lazy, and not continue to look for the way of salvation? Look! The earth is covered in snow, the sky is full of frightening clouds; the wind blows furiously with hostile blasts, and the stormy sea rages. We faint from hunger, and there is no man who can help us. Let us knock at our Lord's gate with prayers, calling on Him, who centuries ago opened a way through the Red Sea for his own people, and miraculously fed them in the wilderness. Let us beg Him to have pity on us in our peril. I believe that, if our faith doesn't fail, He will not leave us hungry on this day of the year, which He himself has made, to fill with so many marvels. I beg you, let's go and look for food, which He may give us so that we can enjoy His festival.'

Saying this, he led them under a cliff, where he used to pray during the night. There they found three pieces of dolphin-meat, that looked as if they had been cut by by human hands, and prepared for cooking. They gave thanks to God on bended knees; then Cuthbert said, 'You see, beloved brothers, how good the grace of God is, to those who trust and hope in the Lord. Look, He has prepared food for his servants. The fact that there are three pieces of meat tells us how many days we will remain here. So take the gifts which Christ has sent us, and eat, and don't be afraid: the sky and the sea will surely be calm on the third day.'

As he predicted, the storm continued with great violence for three days, but was calm on the fourth day, which brought them back with a favourable breeze to their own country.

*The Picts were the ancient inhabitants of what is now north-east Scotland.

12. One day Cuthbert went out of the monastery, accompanied only by a youth, to preach to the people as usual. He began to feel tired from so much walking, and they still had a long way to go before they reached the town that was their destination. Cuthbert tested the lad by saying to him, 'Tell me, where do you expect to find food today? Do you know anyone who lives around here, who could feed you?'

The boy replied, 'I've also been thinking about this, because we didn't bring any food with us. And we don't know anyone along the way who can offer us hospitality. We still have a long way to go, and it will be a hard journey with empty stomachs.'

To this the man of God replied, 'My son, you should learn to always have faith and hope in the Lord. No one who faithfully serves God can ever die of hunger.' And looking up and seeing an eagle flying in the sky, 'Do you see,' he said, 'that eagle flying? It is possible for the Lord to feed us today, even by the help of that bird.'

And so the pair continued talking by the side of a river, when they suddenly saw the eagle sitting on the bank. The man of God said, 'Do you see where the handmaid I spoke about is sitting? Run, and quickly fetch whatever food the Lord has sent us.'

The lad, running off as instructed, brought back a large fish, which the bird had just taken from the river. But the man of God said, 'What have you done, my son? Why have you not given our handmaid her share? Quickly, cut it in two, and give her the helping which she deserves for her service to us.'

The lad did as he was told, and brought back the rest; and when dinner-time came, they went to a nearby village. There they went into a house where the people cooked the fish, and the saint and the boy shared it with the family. It was a very pleasant feast, during which Cuthbert preached the word of God and praised Him for His bounty, for 'Blessed is the man whose hope is the Name of the Lord, and who has not looked to vanity and idle folly.' [paraphrase of Jeremiah 17:7] Resuming their journey, they travelled to the place where Cuthbert intended to teach.

13. As he was preaching to the people of a certain village, Cuthbert suddenly realised that the devil was lurking there, trying to hinder his work. Cuthbert was determined to escape his snares, and he began to teach. As he was preaching, he reminded

his congregation that, 'It is important, my beloved brothers and sisters, that whenever the mysteries of the kingdom of heaven are being preached to you, you should listen carefully with your ears and your hearts. Otherwise the devil, who knows a thousand cunning tricks, might tangle you up with unnecessary worries, and lure you away from the words of eternal salvation.'

Saying this, Cuthbert picked up the thread of his sermon where he had left off. Immediately the devil *seemed* to set fire to a nearby house with a phantom fire, so that sparks seemed to fly through the whole village. The fire was fanned by the wind, and the roaring sound of it filled the air.

Nearly all the people who were listening to Cuthbert, with the exception of a few he kept back with his outstretched hand, leaped up and rushed to fetch water to put out the fire; but real water cannot put out false flames. Only the prayers of Cuthbert could make the devil vanish into empty air, together with his fake fire.

When they saw this, the people felt ashamed, and returned to Cuthbert, begging, on their bended knees, to be forgiven for their silliness, and saying that they now saw that the devil was always trying to lead them astray. And Cuthbert made them all feel strong and steady by continuing to preach to them, as he had been doing before he was interrupted.

14. Cuthbert didn't just put out phantom fires: he also extinguished a real fire with his tears, and this

was a fire which nobody else could put out, even with cold water straight from the well.

As he was travelling round the country, preaching and teaching like the apostles of the New Testament, Cuthbert came to the house of a certain devout woman, a woman he often visited because he knew that she was committed to good works. She had also been his nurse when he was a little boy, and he used to call her his mother.

She had a house, in the western part of a small town which Cuthbert had come to to preach. Suddenly, in the eastern part of the town, a house, which had been set on fire through carelessness, began to burn angrily. Soon a strong easterly wind was blowing off pieces of burning thatch, and scattering them all over the town.

The flames were becoming so hot that they drove away the people who were trying to put out the fire with buckets of water. As soon as she saw what was happening, Cuthbert's old nurse ran to her house and begged the saint to help, before her home, and the whole town, was burned to ashes. But Cuthbert said, 'Cheer up, Mother, and don't be afraid: the fire can't hurt you or your house.'

Then Cuthbert went out and fell flat on the ground in front of the house. He prayed; and as he prayed, the direction of the wind changed. It became a westerly wind, which blew the flames away from the town.

By performing these two fire-miracles, Cuthbert matched the miraculous powers of two of the

Fathers of the Church. By identifying, and putting out, a fantastical fire, he imitated the power of St Benedict, 'who by prayer drove away a seeming fire as it were of a burning kitchen, which had been conjured up before the eyes of his disciples by the craft of the old enemy.'

By turning away the flames of a real fire, he imitated the power of Bishop Marcellinus of Ancona, who, when the city of Ancona itself was burning, fought the fire with his prayers, and put out the flames, which a vast number of the citizens could not put out with water.

Of course, it is not surprising that men who are perfect, and who faithfully serve God, possess the ability to put out fires, since they have already learned to keep down the cravings of their bodies, and 'all the fiery darts of the wicked.' [Ephesians 6:16]

The words of the prophet Isaiah can be applied to such saints: 'when thou walkest through the fire, thou shalt not be burned; neither shall the flame kindle upon thee.' [Isaiah 43:2]

But people like me, who are frail and lazy, know that we dare not try anything of this kind against real fire; and we don't even know if we will be able to avoid the flames of hell after we die.

But the mercy of our Saviour is endless: he gives us unworthy creatures the grace of His protection, so that we can fight the fires of lust in this life, and escape the flames of punishment in the afterlife.

15. We have already seen how Cuthbert could beat the devil's sly tricks: now we will learn how the saint beat the devil in a stand-up fight.

There was a prefect of King Ecgfrid's court, called Hildmaer, whose whole household was devoted to doing good works. For this reason he was a particular favourite of the blessed Cuthbert, and whenever he passed near Hildmaer's house, the saint would visit him.

The wife of this prefect was also fond of charity and the other fruits of goodness, but she was suddenly seized by a devil, and so badly tormented, that she gnashed her teeth, groaned miserably, and threw her arms and legs in all directions. When she behaved like this, she horrified everyone who saw her.

When she lay foaming at the mouth, exhausted and looking as if she was about to die, her husband mounted his horse. He quickly rode to St Cuthbert, and said to him, 'I beg you to send a priest to visit my wife before she dies. She is very ill, and I'm sure she's about to give up the ghost. Please send someone to administer the sacraments of the Body and Blood of our Lord. I also beg you to allow her body to be buried here in the holy place.'

(Hildmaer said this because he was ashamed to admit that she was delirious, when Cuthbert was used to seeing her so calm and serene.)

Cuthbert left Hildmaer for a moment, to think about which priest he should send, but he suddenly learned in spirit, that the prefect's wife was not suffering from a natural illness, but was possessed by a devil. Cuthbert went back to her husband and said, 'I won't send anyone else: I myself will come with you.'

As they travelled to his house, the prefect began to weep, because he was afraid that when Cuthbert found his wife possessed by a devil, he would think that she had not served the Lord with total faith, but with a pretended faith.

But the saint gently comforted him, saying, 'Don't cry: I know that your wife is troubled with a devil; but I also know that before we arrive there, the devil will be scared away, and she will recover. What's more, she herself will joyfully come out to meet us when we arrive, and, in her perfect mind, she shall take these very reins in her hand, and, asking us to enter quickly, she will give us everything we need, as she always does.

'It is not just the wicked who are possessed like this. Because of the hidden judgement of God, innocent people are sometimes held captive by the devil, not only in body, but also in mind.'

While Cuthbert was speaking, they drew near the house, and the wicked spirit suddenly flew away, unable to stand the coming of the Holy Spirit (the saint was full of the Holy Spirit).

The woman's mind was now free of its chains, and she got up, as if she were waking up after a heavy sleep. She went out to welcome Cuthbert, and she held his horse by its bridle, quite recovered in both mind and body. She also begged him to dismount quickly, and to enter, and bless her house. She served him devoutly, and said how, at the first touch of his bridle, she had felt herself freed from her terrible possession.

16. After Cuthbert had spent many years in the monastery of Melrose, and had shown many shining proofs of his spiritual goodness, Eata, his venerable abbot, transferred him to the monastery on the island of Lindisfarne.

He was sent there to teach the monastic way with the authority of a superior, and to illustrate it by setting an example of goodness (at that time Eata governed each of these places as its abbot).

Nobody should be surprised that this little island of Lindisfarne should be, as I have mentioned before, the seat of a bishop, and at the same time, the residence of an abbot and monks – that's just how it is.

The monastery there contains both a bishop and an abbot at the same time, though everyone there is a monk. This is because Aidan, who was the first bishop of Lindisfarne, was himself a monk, and always led a monastic life along with all his people. So after him all the bishops of that place until this day share power just the same. The abbot, who is chosen by the bishop with the agreement of the monks, governs not only the monastery, but all the priests, deacons, chanters, readers, and other ecclesiastical orders, and they all follow the monastic rule, as does the bishop himself.

The blessed Pope Gregory showed how much he loved the monastic way of life, when he wrote to Augustine, whom he had sent as the first bishop of the English. He was replying to a question of Augustine's about how bishops ought to associate with their clergy. Gregory said, among other things, that:

'Because you, my brother, have been instructed in the rules of a monastery, you ought not to live apart from your clergy. You ought to introduce into the church of the English (which has only recently been established) the same mode of life which was in use in the Early Church among our forefathers in the faith. Under that rule, no one had any personal possessions, but everything was shared.'

In this way Cuthbert, on his arrival at the monastery of Lindisfarne, immediately taught the monastic way to the monks, both by the example of his life and by his teaching.

He also did what he always did, which was to stir up the desire of the common people to seek after heavenly things. He did this by frequent visits to the folk who lived nearby.

At this time, he became even more famous for miracles, and healed many sick people through the power of prayer.

He cured some people who were vexed by evil spirits. He did this not only when he was present, by touching them, by prayer, by command, and by exorcism; but even when he wasn't there he cured people by prayer alone, or by predicting their cure. One such case was that of the wife of the prefect, which I have already mentioned.

In the monastery, there were certain monks who chose to carry on their ancient customs, rather than follow the new way. But Cuthbert brought these men round to his way of thinking by the modest power of his patience. By daily practice he brought them, one step at a time, to a better way.

He frequently discussed the rule in the assembly of the brothers*. Whenever he felt he might become worn out by the sharp remarks of the critics of the rule, he would rise up suddenly, and, dismissing the assembly with a placid mind and expression, he would go out.

On the following day, as if he had suffered no opposition the day before, he would repeat the same arguments to the same audience, until by degrees he brought them round.

This shows that he was a man with a special gift of patience, and could put up with any opposition that might appear, whether mental or physical. At the same time he had a cheerful expression, however bad things got, which showed that he was comforted, in times of trouble, by the Holy Spirit.

He was also so enthusiastic about prayer, and so scornful of sleep, that sometimes he went for three or four nights without sleeping at all. Nobody saw him in bed in the monks' dormitory during those nights, and there was nowhere else for him to sleep.

During these sleepless days he either gave

himself up to prayer, alone in some secret place, or worked with his hands (when he wasn't singing psalms) and drove away the drowsiness of sleep by manual labour. Sometimes he would walk round the island, examining each part of it, giving himself some exercise.

He would sometimes criticise the faint-heartedness of the brothers, who didn't like it when they were roused (sometimes with great difficulty) from their slumbers at night or at noon-day. Cuthbert would say, 'No one who wakes me up annoys me – in fact he cheers me up, because he makes me shake off the heaviness of sleep, and gets me ready to do or think something worthwhile.'

Cuthbert was so tender-hearted, and so full of heavenly desires, that when he celebrated the Mass, he could never finish without crying. And when he was celebrating the mysteries of our Lord's Passion, he would get caught up in what he was doing, and offer himself to God with a contrite heart. When the people were standing up for the passage, 'Lift up your hearts,' and 'let us give thanks to our Lord God,' he would lift up his heart instead of his voice, and groan instead of chanting.

He had a strong sense of justice, and would criticise sinners; yet he was meek and modest in pardoning people who were truly sorry. Sometimes, when people were confessing their sins to him, he would be the first to take pity on them, by shedding tears. He was also the first to show by his example how sinners should behave.

His clothing was very ordinary, and he dressed himself so that he was neither remarkably neat nor scruffy. To this day, in the same monastery, no one wears costly, colourful garments, but, following Cuthbert's example, they wear undyed wool.

By these and other examples, Cuthbert persuaded good people to imitate him, and corrected the errors of the stubborn, the wicked and the rebellious.

*In chapter meetings

17. After he had been at the monastery for some years, Cuthbert was happy to be able to retreat to his solitary hermitage; and the best wishes of the abbot and all the monks went with him.

After all his years living an active life, he was delighted to be able to live as a hermit, and turn his mind to quiet thoughts about holy things. He was now like one of those people who are mentioned in Psalm 84: 'They go from strength to strength, every one of them in Zion appeareth before God.'

Ever since he had first learned about the rewards of a hermit's life, Cuthbert had been in the habit of retreating to a solitary place near his cell. There he had learned to fight the devil with the weapons of prayer and fasting. Later, he started to look for a place that was even more isolated.

At last, he chose an island called Farne*. Farne is unlike Lindisfarne, which only becomes an island at high tide: the island Cuthbert chose is about a thousand paces to the east of Lindisfarne, and is always completely surrounded by the sea.

Before Cuthbert came, nobody had been able to live on, let alone raise crops on, this island, because it was infested with demons. But as soon as the saint landed there, armed with the helmet of salvation, the shield of faith, and the sword of the Spirit, which is the Word of God, all the flaming arrows of the devil were put out, and the devil himself, with the whole crowd of his followers, was put to flight.

In this way Cuthbert, the soldier of Christ, became the king of the land he had invaded. He founded a city for his empire, and put up houses for his city. His house was nearly circular, and measured from wall to wall about four or five perches**. From the outside, the walls were taller than a man, but from the inside the walls seemed higher, because the floor was below ground-level, having been cut out of the living rock.

This meant that when Cuthbert looked out of the windows, he could only see the sky. In this way, Cuthbert trained his heart and eyes to desire only heavenly things.

The walls of Cuthbert's house were not made of cut stone, or bricks and mortar, but rough stones and turf which the saint himself had dug out of the centre of the island. Some of these stones were so big that it seemed scarcely possible for four men to lift them. It was discovered that Cuthbert had brought them across the island, and built them into the wall, with the help of angels.

Cuthbert's island home was in two parts; one an oratory***, and the other a living-space. He made the walls of both by digging round, or by cutting out much of the natural earth inside and out; but the roofs were made of rough beams, thatched with straw. There was a larger house at the landing-place of the island, which was used as a guest-house for visiting monks. Not far from this there was a handy spring of water.

*Now called Inner Farne.

**Here Bede uses the *pertica*, a Roman measure of length, which is equivalent to nearly three metres.

***Similar to a chapel: not exactly a church, but a place for prayer and the celebration of the Mass.

18. Although there was water by the guest-house, Cuthbert's own house on the island stood on solid rock, and had no water-supply. For this reason Cuthbert summoned some monks (he had not yet totally hidden himself from visitors). He said to them, 'As you can see, my house has no water. Let us ask God to open a vein of water under this rock, because after all, He "Turned the rock into a standing water, the flint into a fountain of waters." [Psalm 114]

'So let's dig into the middle of the floor of my little house, because I believe that "He will give us to drink of the torrent of his pleasure" ' [paraphrase of part of Psalm 36]

They dug a pit, and the next day they found it

full of water, welling up from below. It was beyond doubt that this water was drawn out of that very dry and hard ground by the prayers of the saint. By a miracle, it always exactly filled its basin, so that it never wet the floor by bubbling over, though the basin was never empty. God regulated the supply so well that it was never more nor less than what was needed.

Once he had built his house, with help from the monks, Cuthbert the man of God began to live alone. At first, though, when the monks came to visit him, he used to come out of his cell and greet them. He would wash their feet with warm water, and sometimes he felt obliged to take off his own shoes and allow them to wash *his* feet. This wasn't easy, because he cared nothing for his body, and sometimes he wouldn't take off his stockings (which were made of animal skins) for several months. In fact it is likely that he would sometimes only take his stockings off once a year, at Easter, for the ceremony of the washing of the feet on Maundy Thursday.

Because he was constantly kneeling to pray with his hide stockings on, it was discovered that on one foot he had a large callous where the leg met the foot.

Soon Cuthbert's desire for perfection increased, and he shut himself up in his little monastery and learned to lead a solitary life. There he fasted, prayed, and denied himself sleep, and seldom talked to anyone who came to visit. At first he would open his window so that he could see, and be seen by, visiting monks, but eventually he only opened it to give his blessing, or when he really couldn't avoid opening it.

19. At the beginning of his time as a hermit, Cuthbert accepted a little bread to eat from the monks, and drank water from his spring, but later he thought it would be better to live by the work of his own hands, like the Fathers of the Church. So he asked the monks to bring him some gardening tools, and some wheat to sow. He sowed the wheat in spring, but by midsummer nothing had grown.

When the monks visited him again he said to them, 'Perhaps there's something wrong with the soil, or perhaps it is the will of God, but wheat just won't grow here. Next time, please bring some barley seeds: perhaps barley will grow. If God won't let that grow either, I should return to the monastery, rather than remain here and rely on other people's work.'

So they brought him some barley, which he sowed a long time after the proper season for sowing. When it seemed impossible that it would grow, it produced a bumper crop.

But as it was beginning to ripen, flocks of birds came and fed on the barley. Cuthbert used to tell people how he got rid of them: it was in his nature to tell stories about himself, to strengthen other people's faith.

He approached the birds and asked them, 'Why

do you eat the grain you have not sown yourselves? Do you think you have more need of it than I do? If God has told you to do this, do it, but if not, go away, and eat someone else's crop.'

He had hardly finished speaking before the whole flock flew off, and they never attacked his harvest again. In this way, Cuthbert imitated the actions of two of the Fathers of the Church; by making a spring of water come from a rock, he was imitating St Benedict, although Benedict made a larger spring, to quench the thirst of more people. By driving the birds away from his harvest, Cuthbert was following in the footsteps of St Antony, who by a single word stopped the wild asses from ruining the little garden he had planted.

20. The next miracle is another one where Cuthbert imitated St Benedict. This miracle also shows how the behaviour of birds can show up human pride and stubbornness.

Two crows often visited Cuthbert's island, and one day the saint noticed that they were taking straw from the roof of his guest-house to build their nest. To stop them, Cuthbert made a gentle movement of his hand, and said, 'In the name of Jesus Christ, leave this place, and don't come back here, where you have done such harm.'

Immediately, the birds left, though they were very sad to go. Three days later one of them returned, and, finding the saint digging, he landed in front of him, spread out his wings, bowed his head, made a noise, and seemed to be begging for forgiveness.

At this, Cuthbert, who understood crow-language, gave him permission to return to the island. The bird immediately flew off to fetch his companion, and both of them returned and brought a gift: half a flitch of fat bacon. The saint used to show this to the monks who came to see him. He let them use it to grease their shoes, and reminded them how a proud bird had humbled itself to find forgiveness.

To teach people a lesson about how they might improve themselves, the birds in question remained on the island for many years, building their nests but never annoying anyone.

If anyone finds it absurd to learn a lesson of goodness from birds, they should remember Solomon, who said, 'Go to the ant, thou sluggard; consider her ways, and be wise.' [Proverbs 6:6]

21. Not only did the birds of the air and the creatures of the sea serve the saint, but even the sea itself helped him, like the air and the fire, as we have seen. And it's not surprising that every creature helped him, because he served the Creator of all the creatures with his whole heart. (Most of us cannot expect to have Cuthbert's command of the elements, because we don't serve their Creator as Cuthbert did).

As I say, the sea itself served Christ's servant when he needed help.

When he started to build a little hut for himself in his monastery, he chose a spot by the sea, where the constant dashing of the waves had hollowed out the rock into a deep and narrow cleft. This cleft was about twelve feet wide, so the foundation of Cuthbert's hut would need to be the same width.

So he asked the monks to bring a piece of wood twelve feet long, when they next came to visit him. This they promised to do, but after they had received his blessing and left for home, they forgot his request, and didn't have the wood with them when they came back.

On this occasion, Cuthbert greeted the monks kindly, commended them to God and asked, 'So where's the piece of timber I asked you to bring?' Then the monks remembered, admitted they had forgotten, and asked the saint to forgive them.

Cuthbert wasn't angry: he spoke to them gently, and invited them stay on the island and rest till morning, saying, 'I believe that God, at least, will not forget what I need.'

The monks stayed the night, and when they got up early in the morning they saw that the tide had washed up a wooden beam of exactly the right size, and even laid it on shore at the very place where it was needed. When they saw this, the monks were amazed that a man could be so holy that even the sea would serve him. They blamed themselves again for their forgetfulness – it seemed to them that the sea had shown them how to behave.

22. Cuthbert became so famous that a great many people came to visit him, not just from Lindisfarne but even from the remotest corners of Britain. They came to confess their sins, to tell the saint about the demons that troubled them, and to hear Cuthbert's kind words when they were in trouble. Nobody was disappointed: when they had spoken to Cuthbert, all their worries seemed to go away.

Cuthbert knew how to use holy words to refresh the spirit of anyone who had suffered a bereavement. He also knew how to remind troubled people of the promise of heaven, and to show them how both happiness and joy quickly pass. And he knew all about the temptations that the devil uses to trap people.

He explained to people how a soul that had no love of God or other people could easily be trapped, and showed how complete faith could help people escape the devil's traps as easily as a man might walk through a spider's web.

'I've often been thrown off cliffs by demons,' he would say, 'and have been pelted with stones and shown all sorts of temptations and horrors, designed to drive me off my island battlefield; but I've never been injured, or even afraid.'

When speaking to his fellow-monks, Cuthbert humbly reminded them that his solitary way of life was not more holy than the life of a monk in a monastery.

'Life in a monastery is more holy,' he said,

'because there every part of a man's life is subject to the command of the abbot, who tells him when to pray, fast, keep vigil or work with his hands.

'I have known many cloistered monks who were far holier than I am: some were like prophets. One of those was the venerable Abbot Boisil of Melrose. Years ago, when he was a very old man, he brought me up at his monastery. He prophesied about me, and everything he predicted has happened – except one thing. In this one thing, I hope he was mistaken.'

By this Cuthbert meant Boisil's prediction that he, Cuthbert, would become a bishop. Cuthbert didn't like the idea of this at all: it troubled him, because he wanted to carry on living the life of a hermit.

23. Even when he was living alone and had little contact with people, Cuthbert never stopped performing miraculous cures.

An abbess called Elfled, who loved Cuthbert, went down with a chronic illness that left her unable to stand or walk, and forced her to crawl about on all fours like an animal. Her illness *had* been much worse, and had even threatened her life, but divine grace had helped her, although the doctors couldn't: now her only problem was standing and walking.

Elfled was a virgin of royal birth, and ruled over the many nuns in her care in a way that added lustre to her noble name.

Her symptoms lasted so long that she began to

fear that her weakness would be permanent: she had long since despaired of getting any remedy from her doctors.

One day, troubled by sad thoughts, she thought of Cuthbert and his quiet, holy way of life. She said, 'I wish I had something belonging to my dear Cuthbert, because I know, and I trust in the Lord, that I would soon be healed by it!'

Not long after, someone arrived with a linen girdle, which Cuthbert had sent as a present to Elfled. She was very pleased by the gift, and, knowing that her longing for a cure had already been communicated to the holy man by heaven, she put the girdle on. Next morning she was able to stand up straight, and on the third day she was restored to perfect health. I learned this story from Herefrid, a priest of the church of Lindisfarne.

A few days later, one of the nuns in the same monastery began to suffer from an unbearable pain in her head. Every day, her pain increased, and she seemed close to death. Her venerable abbess came to visit her, and when she saw her so terribly ill, she took Cuthbert's girdle and ordered that it be bound round the nun's head. Soon the pain disappeared altogether, and she was completely healed by the end of the day.

She took off the girdle, and put it in a box; but when the abbess asked her for it, some days later, it was no longer there: in fact, it had gone forever. Obviously, this happened because of divine intervention: God wanted to prove by two miracles of healing that Cuthbert was a holy man – after these miracles, nobody could doubt that any more.

And the girdle had to disappear, because otherwise all sorts of sick people would flock to it to be cured. And if some person who was not worthy to be healed was not healed, then people might question whether the girdle really was miraculous.

24. Later, Abbess Elfled sent a message to Cuthbert, asking him to come and talk to her about some important business. So the saint boarded a ship, accompanied by some brother monks, and sailed to the island of Coquet: an island so named because it lies at the mouth of the river of the same name.

The island is celebrated for its community of monks; it was there that Elfled had arranged to meet Cuthbert.

The abbess was well-satisfied with the saint's replies to her many questions; but she suddenly fell at his feet, and begged him by the terrible and venerable Name of the heavenly King and His angels, to tell her how much longer King Ecgfrid, her brother, would live and rule over the kingdom of the Angles.

'I ask you because I know,' she said, 'that you have the power to see the future, and can answer my question.'

Cuthbert trembled at her question, and did not want to answer it. 'It is amazing,' he said, 'that you, a woman who is wise, and knowledgeable about the holy Scriptures, should speak about a man's life as if it were long, because, as the Psalm says, "Our years are reckoned as a spider's web." [paraphrase of Job 8:14]

'Doesn't Solomon warn us that, "If a man live many years,and rejoice in them all; yet let him remember the days of darkness; for they shall be many." [Ecclesiastes 11:8] When a man has only one more year to live, won't his whole life seem short?'

When the abbess heard this prediction, she cried floods of tears. Having wiped her face, her feminine boldness then made her beg Cuthbert to tell her who would succeed the king, since he had neither sons nor brothers?

Cuthbert was silent for moment, then he said, 'Don't say that he doesn't have sons, because he shall have a successor: someone you will be able to embrace, as you would Ecgfrid himself, as a sister.' But she said, 'Tell me, I beg you, where is this successor now?'

Cuthbert said, 'You see this mighty ocean, and you know how many islands are in it? It is easy for God to find a king of the Angles from among these islands!'

From these words, Elfled knew that Cuthbert was talking about Aldfrith, who was said to be the son of Ecgfrid's father. At that time Aldfrith lived in exile, for the sake of his education, on one of the Scottish islands.

Now Elfled knew that Ecgfrid wanted to make Cuthbert a bishop, and, wishing to discover whether this would happen, she said, 'Oh! how the hearts of mortals are confused by different intentions! Some enjoy the riches that they have, while others, loving riches, are never satisfied. You have neglected the glory of the world, though it is offered to you; and although you might have the great honour of becoming a bishop, you prefer your retreat in the wilderness.'

Cuthbert said, 'I know that I am not worthy of such a high rank; nevertheless, I can't escape the commands of the Ruler of heaven. If He has decided that I should bear that burden, I believe that He will restore me to freedom shortly after. Perhaps, after not more than two years, he will send me back to my beloved solitude. But I command you, in the Name of our Lord and Saviour, not to tell anyone what you have heard here until after my death.'

When he had answered more of her questions, and taught her what she longed to know, he returned to his island monastery, and continued his solitary life.

A little later, a well-attended synod met in the presence of the very pious King Ecgfrid, whom God loved. The synod was chaired by Archbishop Theodore of blessed memory. At this synod, Cuthbert was unanimously elected Bishop of Lindisfarne.

Many messengers and letters were sent to him, but he could not be dragged from his retreat. So the king himself, with the holy priest Trumwine, and many other religious and honourable men, sailed to the island. There they all knelt down, and with tears in their eyes they begged Cuthbert to consent. And they didn't give up until they drew him, also crying, from his beloved hermitage, and dragged him before the synod.

When he got there, Cuthbert reluctantly agreed to accept the great responsibility. In this way, he bowed to the unanimous will of the whole synod.

His consecration did not follow immediately: this had to wait until winter had passed.

This was all in line with Cuthbert's prophecies, as was the killing of King Ecgfrid, which happened a year later. Ecgfrid was killed by the the Picts. Aldfrid, his illegitimate brother, who had been living in voluntary exile for the sake of his education, now succeeded Ecgfrid as king.

III. Cuthbert Becomes a Bishop

25. After he was made a bishop, Cuthbert returned to his island, where he continued, for at time, to wrestle in secret for the Lord, with his usual devotion. Then Eata, the venerable bishop, summoned him to a conference with himself at Melrose.

As he was returning home from this interview, a certain earl of King Ecgfrid met him, and begged him to come and give a blessing to his village and his household. When he arrived, and had been greeted in a friendly way by everyone, the earl told Cuthbert about one of his servants, who was ill.

The earl said, 'I thank God, holy father, that you have come to visit us. We all believe that your visit will be good for both our souls and our bodies. For a very long time now, my servant has been suffering from a serious illness. Today he is so bad that he seems more like a dying man than a sick one. In fact, the lower part of his body seems to be dead already, and the only way we can tell that he is still alive is the faint breath from his mouth and nostrils.'

Cuthbert immediately blessed some water, and gave it to a servant of the earl, whose name was Baldhelm. (He is living to this day, and is now a priest in the church of Lindisfarne. There he lives a holy life, and thinks it is sweeter than honey to re-tell the miracle-stories of the man of God to everyone who wants to hear them. He told me about the miracle which I am now describing.)

Giving the blessed water to Baldhelm, Cuthbert said, 'Go, and give this to the sick man to taste.' Baldhelm took it, and poured it into the patient's mouth three times. The third time, the sick man fell into a deep and tranquil sleep, to everyone's surprise. This was in the evening, and he passed the night peacefully. His master, visiting him next morning, found that he was completely cured.

26. The venerable Cuthbert was an excellent bishop, and followed the example of the apostles by doing good works. He protected his flock with constant prayer, and inspired them to thoughts of heaven with helpful advice. And he did what every teacher should do – he taught by example.

He rescued friendless people from the actions of powerful people, and saved poor people from harsh treatment. He worked hard to comfort the depressed and feeble-minded, but he also made people who enjoyed doing mischief feel sad about what they had done.

He continued to practice self-denial, and though he was surrounded by people, he continued to live the hard life of a monk.

He gave food to the hungry, he gave clothing to those who were shivering with cold, and all his life was filled with other signs which showed him to be a true bishop. Miracles, such as those we have already described, continued to show his inner goodness; the goodness of the soul, as well as his more obvious outer goodness.

27. Soon King Ecgfrid was rashly leading his army against the Picts, and devastating their kingdom with ferocious cruelty.

Cuthbert knew that what he had predicted was soon to happen, that is, that this king was soon to die. So he went to the city of Carlisle to speak to the queen, who was there waiting for news of the war, living in her sister's monastery.

Next day, as some of the inhabitants were showing him the walls of the city, and also a marvellous fountain left behind by the Romans, Cuthbert suddenly became troubled in spirit, leaned on his staff and looked down at the ground. Then he stood up straight, lifted his eyes to heaven, groaned deeply, and softly muttered, 'Perhaps at this very moment the battle has ended.'

A priest who was standing nearby understood what he was talking about and blurted out, 'How do you know that?' But Cuthbert didn't want to say more than he had said, and he asked, 'Don't you see how amazingly changed and disturbed the air is? And who among mortals can understand the judgements of God?'

Nevertheless, the saint went straight to the queen and spoke to her in secret (this happened on a

Saturday). He said to her, 'See that you mount your chariot at dawn on Monday (because you can't ride it on a Sunday) and go as quickly as possible to the royal city, in case the king has been killed. Tomorrow, I'm dedicating the church of a nearby monastery, but I will follow you straight after that.'

The next day, Cuthbert preached to the monks of the same monastery. When he had finished his preaching, which was very well received, he added, 'I beg you, most beloved brothers, according to the warning of the apostle, to "Watch ye, stand fast in the faith, quit you like men, be strong." [1 Corinthians 16:13] I don't want some temptation to come along and find you unprepared. So you should always remember that saying of the Lord, "Watch ye and pray, lest ye enter into temptation." ' [Mark 14:38]

The people who were listening thought that Cuthbert was talking about the plague, which had recently killed some of the monks, and had already spread far and wide. But Cuthbert continued, 'Once, when I was living as a hermit on my island, some of the monks came to me, on Christmas Day. They begged me to come out of my poor little house and spend that special day with them.

'So I went out, and we sat down to the feast. But in the middle of the meal I said to them, "I beg you, brothers, to be careful, in case you become over-confident and surrender to some temptation."

'But they answered, "Let's be joyful today: it's the birthday of our Lord Jesus Christ."

'And I said, "Well, let it be so." A little later, still during the meal, as we were talking happily, I warned them again that we should be serious in prayer and staying awake, and be prepared for all the attacks of temptation.

'But they said, "You teach us well, yes, very well, but we always have many days of fasting and prayer and staying awake, so let's rejoice in the Lord today. Didn't the angels announce good news of great joy to the shepherds, when our Lord was born? Good news for all the people?"

'And I said, "Well, let us do so." As we continued eating, and were spending the day in joy, I repeated for the third time the same words of advice, and they understood that there was a reason why I had advised them like that. They were very worried, and said, "Let's do what you recommend: we need to be ready to look out for the snares of the devil."

'When this happened, none of us knew that we would be attacked by a new temptation; but I knew by instinct that the heart should always be defended against the sudden storms of temptation.

'In the morning, after they left me to return to their monastery, (that is, to Lindisfarne) they found that one of their brothers had died of plague during the night.

'The plague spread and grew worse every day for months, and almost a whole year, so that nearly the whole of that noble community of spiritual fathers and brothers went to God. This shows that we should all stay awake and pray, and be ready for any disaster.'

When Cuthbert had said all this, the monks thought, as I said before, that he was warning them about a return of the plague. But next day, the truth was revealed when a survivor of the battle arrived. It turned out that King Ecgfrid and his entire bodyguard had been killed at the precise moment when Cuthbert, standing by the fountain, had sensed that this had happened.

28. Not long after this, the saint was invited to Carlisle again, to ordain some priests, and to give his blessing to the queen, who was to become a nun.

There was a holy priest called Herbert, who had long been a spiritual friend of Cuthbert. This man led a solitary life, on an island in the vast lake which is the source of the river Derwent. He would come every year to listen to Cuthbert preach on the subject of everlasting salvation.

On hearing that his friend was in Carlisle, he joined him there, as usual, in the hope of being inspired to heavenly desires by Cuthbert's preaching. While these two were speaking wisely together, Cuthbert said, among other things, 'Brother Herbert, if you have anything to ask me, ask me now, because after we have parted this time, we shall never see each other again in this world. I am convinced that the time of my death is not far off, when I will leave this body.'

On hearing this, Herbert fell at the saint's feet, and, dropping tears from his eyes, he said, 'I beg you in the name of God, don't leave me. Remember me, and beg heaven to let us go to that place, and see God, together.

'You know how I have always tried to live as you advised me. When I went wrong, it was only through ignorance or weakness, and I have always done what you instructed.'

Bishop Cuthbert bowed down in prayer, and quickly knew that his prayer had been heard. 'Get up, my brother,' he said, 'and don't cry. Be happy, because your prayer has been answered.'

Things turned out exactly as Cuthbert had promised. After separating from each other, they never saw each other again in this world. They died at exactly the same time, and the angels took them both up to heaven. But before that could happen, Herbert had to suffer a long and painful illness, which was good for his soul. This illness made Herbert's soul as good as Cuthbert's, so that when they both died at the same time, they could travel together to the same part of heaven.

29. One day, Cuthbert was going round his diocese, teaching the people of the villages and cottages about salvation. He was also laying his hands on people who had recently been baptised, so that they could receive the grace of the Holy Spirit.

He came to the mansion of a certain earl, whose wife was lying sick, and was almost at the point of death. The nobleman, coming out to meet Cuthbert, gave thanks to God, on his knees, for the saint's arrival. Leading him in, he welcomed him with kind hospitality.

After he had washed Cuthbert's hands and feet, and the saint had sat down again, the earl began to tell him about the hopeless illness of his wife. He begged him to bless some water that could be sprinkled on her.

'Because I believe,' he said, 'that soon, by the gift of God, she will either be cured, or, if she dies, that she will pass from death to everlasting life. By dying, she will enter more quickly into the reward that awaits her, after her long illness.'

The saint agreed to do as he was asked. He blessed some water and gave it to a priest, ordering him to sprinkle the patient with it. The priest entered her bed-chamber, where she lay half-dead, sprinkled her and her bed, and opened her mouth, to pour in some of the water.

The result was astounding! As soon as the blessed water touched the sick woman (who was quite unaware of what had been done) she was restored so completely to health, both of mind and body, that she immediately came to her perfect mind. She blessed the Lord and gave thanks to Him, Who had sent such a guest to visit her, and cure her.

Without delay, rising up in perfect health, she went to serve Cuthbert and the priest. It was good to see how a woman who had avoided drinking from the cup of death, by the blessing of the saint, became the first to offer him a drink.

In this way, she imitated the example of the

mother-in-law of the apostle Peter, who, on being cured of a fever by our Lord, rose up and served Him and His disciples. [Mark 1:29-33]

30. This miracle was similar to another cure performed by Cuthbert, the venerable bishop. Many people witnessed this, including a pious priest called Ethelwold, who was then Cuthbert's chaplain (he is now abbot of the monastery of Melrose).

As usual, Cuthbert was travelling among the people, preaching to them, when he came to a certain town. Here there were a small number of nuns who had fled from their monastery because they feared a barbarian army. The saint had given the nuns this town as a place to live.

One of the nuns, who was related to Ethelwold, the priest I have just mentioned, was suffering from a terrible illness. For a whole year, she had endured unbearable pains in her head, and all down one side, and the doctors had given up on her.

When Cuthbert's travelling companions had told the saint about her case, they begged him to cure her. Taking pity on her terrible state of health, Cuthbert anointed her with consecrated oil. She immediately started to get better, and in a few days she was restored to perfect health.

31. We should also remember another miracle which was done by Cuthbert, although it was done in his absence. We have already mentioned Hildmaer the prefect, whose wife had been exorcised by the saint.

Later, this same Hildmaer became more and more ill himself, and had to stay in bed. He really seemed to be at the point of death.

Several of his friends gathered round to comfort the sick man, and as they were seated by his bed, one of them happened to mention that he had a loaf with him, which Cuthbert had just given him, after he had blessed it.

'I believe,' said he, 'that if Hildmaer ate some of this, it would cure him, as long as our faith is strong.' (None of them were priests or monks, but they were all believers.)

Each of them then said in turn that they believed that Hildmaer could be cured by the blessed bread. They filled a cup with water, put a little piece of the loaf into it, and gave it to Hildmaer to drink.

As soon as Hildmaer had swallowed the water, which was made holy by the bread, his pain disappeared, and his arms and legs stopped wasting away. Not long after that, he was restored to health and strength. The speed of this unexpected cure inspired the hearts not only of himself and his friends, but also everyone who saw or heard of it. The news made them praise the holiness of Cuthbert, the servant of Christ, and marvel at the goodness and trueness of his faith.

32. Once Cuthbert, the holy shepherd, was doing the rounds of his sheepfold when he came to a wild, mountainous district. Here he planned to place his hands on anyone who met him at a certain place and

time. These people had journeyed to meet Cuthbert from many scattered little villages in that part of the world.

There was no church there, or any other building fit for a bishop and his companions, so tents had been put up by the side of the road. The people themselves sheltered in temporary huts made of branches from a nearby forest. Here the saint preached the Word, to the crowds that flocked to hear him, for two whole days. He also placed his hands on people who had recently been baptised, giving them the gift of the Holy Spirit.

Suddenly some women appeared out of the forest, carrying a young man on a litter. The man was wasting away because of a long, miserable illness. The women set him down at the edge of the forest, and sent to the bishop to ask if they could bring the youth to him.

When the boy had been brought to Cuthbert, and the saint saw how ill he was, he ordered everyone to back off and leave him alone with the young man. Cuthbert armed himself with prayer and gave the youth his blessing. Immediately the sickness, which the doctors had been unable to cure with their various concoctions, vanished completely.

Within the hour, the youth got up, ate some food and gave thanks to God. He rejoined the women who had carried him there, and although they had brought him to Cuthbert a sick young man, they all went home in joy, and in perfect health.

33. At that time, the plague came to these parts. It killed so many people, that in many large towns, estates and villages there were few or no people left alive. Because of this, Cuthbert constantly toured round his diocese, preaching and bringing comfort to the survivors.

When he arrived at a certain village, and had preached to the people, he said to his priest, 'Do you think that there is anyone left alive in this area, who needs a visit from us, or have we visited all the sick people, and should we now start on the others?'

The priest, looking round, saw a woman standing some distance away. She had lost one son, and was now holding up his brother, who was very near death. Her tears were rolling down her cheeks, and you could see how much she was grieving.

As soon as the priest had pointed her out, Cuthbert went towards her, gave his blessing, kissed the child, and said to his mother, 'Don't be afraid, and don't be sad. This child of yours will recover, and live; and nobody else in your house will die of the plague.'

The child lived for a long time after this, and his mother told everybody about what Cuthbert had done.

34. By this time, Cuthbert knew that he himself was nearing death. He decided to give up being a bishop, and return to a solitary life. Alone on his island, he would have time to pray and sing psalms, and

concentrate his thoughts on his future life in heaven.

But first he planned to visit his entire diocese, and even preach to faithful people outside it, before he returned to the hermit's life.

He had been invited to the monastery of the aforementioned abbess Elfled, so he went to this large monastery to talk to her, and to dedicate a church.

As they sat at dinner, Cuthbert suddenly turned his mind away from the meal, to thoughts of spiritual things. His whole body became loose, the colour of his face changed, his eyes were unusually agitated, and he dropped the knife he had been holding.

His priest, who had been serving him his dinner, noticed this. He said to the abbess, 'Ask the bishop what he has just seen: I can tell that he has seen something spiritual, which the rest of us can't see.'

Elfled turned to Cuthbert and said, 'I beg you, my lord bishop, tell me what you have just seen.' But Cuthbert tried to pretend that he hadn't seen anything, and said playfully, 'Do you think I'm able to eat all day? Surely I should rest a little now.' The abbess, however, pressed him to tell her about his vision. At last he said, 'I have seen the soul of a certain holy person borne up by angels to the joys of heaven.'

'From what place was he taken?' asked Elfled.

'From your monastery.'

'And who was it?'

'Tomorrow, when I am celebrating Mass, you yourself will tell me his name.'

On hearing this, the abbess immediately sent to the larger of her monasteries, to see whether anyone had died. But the messenger, finding all safe and well there, set out next morning to return to his mistress. On the road he met some people who were carrying the dead body of a monk to burial, in a cart. The messenger asked who it was, and was told that it was a shepherd, a good man, who had foolishly climbed a tree, fallen down, and was so badly injured that he died. This happened at the same moment that Cuthbert had seen his soul going up to heaven.

The messenger told the abbess what had happened, and she immediately went to the bishop, who was then dedicating the church.

'I beg you, my lord bishop,' she said, astonished at her own words, 'that you will remember the soul of my servant Hadwald during Mass. He died yesterday, after falling from a tree.'

This showed everyone how much of the spirit of prophecy was present in the heart of the saint. Not only could he see the soul of a dead man going up to heaven: he could also predict how he would hear the news of the man's death.

35. After he had toured all the mountainous districts, Cuthbert came to that monastery of nuns which, as I mentioned before, was not far from the mouth of the river Tyne. Here he was honourably received by that

most noble servant of Christ, Werca the abbess.

After they had woken up from the noonday rest, Cuthbert, feeling thirsty, asked for something to drink. They asked him what he would like to drink? Wine or beer?

'Give me water,' he said, and they offered him water which they had drawn from the spring. When he had blessed it, and drunk a little, he handed it to his priest, who was standing beside him, and he gave it to a servant.

Having taken the cup, the servant, who was the priest of the monastery, said, 'Can I drink from the same cup as the bishop?' Cuthbert's priest replied, 'Yes, why not?'

So the priest drank, but the water seemed to him to taste like wine. To make sure, he handed the cup to a monk who was standing nearby. The pair looked at each other in astonishment, and later agreed that they had never tasted better wine. This story was told to me by one of those men, who lived for a long time in our monastery at the mouth of the river Wear, and is now buried there.

36. Having spent two years as a bishop, Cuthbert knew that he was soon to die. So he threw off the burden of the bishop's job, and returned as soon as possible to the challenge of a hermit's life, which he loved so much. He did this so that the flame of his old contrition would consume the thorns of worldly care which had grown up inside him.

In the early days, he would leave his house and

talk face to face with the monks who came to visit him.

One day, several monks stopped by, and Cuthbert went out to them. He refreshed them with holy words, then said, 'It is time for me to return to my cell. I can see that you are ready to set out, but you must eat first. Take this goose, cook it and eat it. When you have finished, get in your boat and return home.'

When he had said this, Cuthbert prayed, blessed the monks and returned to his own cell. The others did eat, as they had been told to do, but as they had plenty of their own food with them, they left Cuthbert's goose hanging against the wall.

After they had eaten, and were preparing to get into their boat, a terrible storm blew up, and prevented them from putting to sea.

For seven days they remained trapped on the island by the boiling waves; nevertheless, it didn't occur to them that they were stuck there because they had disobeyed Cuthbert.

When they spoke to the saint, and complained about their delay, he tried to teach them patience. On the seventh day, he went out to them to cheer them up with a visit. When he entered the house where they were staying, and saw that the goose had not been eaten, he calmly pointed out how they had disobeyed, saying, 'Is this goose still hanging there uneaten? No wonder the sea won't let you leave! Put it straight into the pot, cook it and eat it. Then the sea will calm down, and you'll be able to return home.'

They immediately did as he told them, and as soon as the goose began to boil in the pot, both the sea and the wind grew calm. As soon as they had finished their meal, they got into their boat and sailed home.

They crossed the sea with joy, but also with shame. They were ashamed of their disobedience and slow-wittedness – they had failed to see how God was punishing them. But they were also glad to have seen how God loved Cuthbert so much that He used the elements themselves to punish those who ignored his instructions. They were also pleased to recall that God had taken the trouble to communicate with them through a miracle.

I didn't learn about this miracle at second hand: I heard the story from one of the monks who was there. I mean Cynemund, a monk of venerable life, and a priest of the same monastery. Today he is known to many of the faithful, and is as celebrated for the grace of his good life as for his great age.

IV. Cuthbert's Last Days

37. Cuthbert returned to his cell on the island, shortly after Christmas.

A crowd of monks stood around him as he was going aboard his ship. One of them was an old monk who had lived a very Christian life, whose faith was strong, but who was now physically very weak because he suffered from dysentery.

He asked Cuthbert, 'Tell us, lord bishop, when will we see you again?'

Cuthbert, who knew the truth, answered his simple question, saying, 'When you bring my body back here.'

Cuthbert passed nearly two months, enjoying the peaceful life to which he had returned, and training both his body and his mind. Then he went down with a sudden illness. The pain of this prepared him for the joys of heaven.

I will describe his death, the details of which I heard about from Herefrid, a devout priest, who was then abbot at the monastery of Lindisfarne.

'Cuthbert died after three weeks of an illness that made him waste away. He became ill on the fourth day of the week, and he also departed to the Lord on the fourth day of the week.

'I came to him on the first morning after he was taken ill (I had gone to the island with some monks three days before). I went to ask for his blessing and instruction, and when he realised that I had arrived, Cuthbert came to his window. Instead of saying hello, he merely sighed.

'Of course I asked, "What's the matter, my lord bishop? Have you become ill overnight?"

'He said, "Yes, sickness has stricken me."

'I was thinking of his old illness, which had troubled him every day. This disease always made him waste away, and I didn't think he was speaking about any new illness.

'Without asking any more questions I said, "Give us your blessing, because it is time for us to go on board and return home."

' "Yes, go on board and return home safe," he said, "and when God has taken my soul, bury me in this cell, at the south side of my oratory, opposite the east side of the Holy Cross which I have put up there. On the north of the oratory you'll find a stone coffin, hidden under the earth, which was a gift from Abbot Cudda. Put my body in that, and wrap it in the fine linen which you will find there. I didn't want to wear it during my life, but for the love of Abbess Werca, who gave it to me, I have taken care to save it to act as my shroud."

'Then I said, "I beg you, father, let some of the monks remain here and look after you, if you think you are dying."

'But he said, "Go now, but come back at a suitable time."

'Though I begged him more earnestly to accept our service, I was unable to make him agree. At last I asked him when we could return, and he said, "When God pleases, He will show you."

'So we followed his orders and went away, and when I had gathered all the monks together in the church, I ordered them to pray for him all day and all night. I told them that it seemed to me from what he had said to me, that he was soon to depart to God.

'Because of his illness, I was very anxious to get back to him, but for five days a storm prevented me. We could not go back to Cuthbert's island, and we found out later that God Himself had stopped us. God wanted His servant to suffer the pain of illness and isolation, so that he would have a keener battle against the flesh and the devil.

'When calm weather returned, we went back to the island, where we found that Cuthbert had left his monastery, and was sitting in the guest-house.

'An urgent matter forced the monks who had come with me to sail back to the opposite shore. But I remained on the island, and decided that I should see to our father's needs.

'I warmed some water and washed his foot, which had been swollen for a long time, and now had a suppurating ulcer, which needed attention. I also warmed some wine and brought it to him, and asked him to taste it. I saw by his face that he was exhausted by hunger and sickness. When I had finished, he laid himself quietly on his bed, and I sat down beside him.

'To break the silence, I said, "I see, my lord bishop, that you have been very ill since we left you. When we left before, why wouldn't you let us leave some monks behind to nurse you?"

'He said, "This has happened by the will of God. He wanted me to suffer alone. That's why my disease became worse just after you left me. That's why I left my cell and came here to the guest-house, so that if anybody came to look after me, he wouldn't have to go into my cell.

' "Since then I haven't moved from my seat, or changed the position of my limbs. I have just been sitting here quietly, for five days and nights."

'I said, "My lord bishop, how can you live like this? Haven't you even had any food?"

'Then he lifted up the covering of the bed where he was sitting and showed me five onions hidden there. "This has been my food," he said: "as soon as my mouth becomes dry, I refresh myself with a taste of one of these." (One of the onions looked half-eaten.)

' "My enemies have never tempted me as much as they have during these five days," he went on. I didn't dare to ask what these temptations were: I only asked him to let some of us look after him. He said yes to this, and several monks stayed with him, including one called Bede* who had often served him.

98

'He particularly wanted Bede to remain behind because he knew about everything Cuthbert had been given, either as a gift or a loan. The saint wanted to be sure to return everything to its rightful owner, before his own death.

'Cuthbert also named another monk whom he wanted to remain behind: this was the man who had suffered from diarrhoea for a long time, and whose case had baffled the doctors. He was a pious, prudent and grave man, who deserved to be a witness to the last days of Cuthbert, and to hear his last words.

'At home, I told the monks that our venerable father had given orders that he should be buried on his own island. "But it seems to me," I added, "that it would be much better for us to ask him to let his body be moved here, to the church."

'Everyone agreed, so we went back to the bishop and said, "We dare not, lord bishop, ignore your wish to be buried here; nevertheless, it seems good to us to ask permission to transfer your body, so that we can have you with us."

'But he said, "It is my wish to rest here, where I have fought my little wrestling-match for the Lord. I want to finish my life here, and I hope to be raised up from here by the merciful Judge to a crown of righteousness. And I think it would be better for you if I rest here, because of all the wicked people who will seek sanctuary at my tomb, because they will have been told that I was a servant of Christ during my life. These seekers of sanctuary will cause you a lot of trouble: you will have to intercede for them with the powerful people of the world."

'But after we had begged him continually, and for a long time, and assured him that work of this kind would be both light and agreeable to us, Cuthbert took counsel with himself and replied, "If you really want to change my plans, and carry my body from this place, you should bury me inside your church, so that you can visit my tomb whenever you please, and have it in your power to let in, or not let in, any visitors."

'We knelt down and thanked him for his consent and for his advice, then returned home, though from that time we visited him frequently.

*This is not Bede the author.

38. 'As his sickness continued, Cuthbert saw that the time of his death was at hand, and he commanded that he should be carried back to his little cell and oratory. This was at nine in the morning. We carried him there, because he was too weak to walk. But when we came to the door, we begged him to allow one of us to go in with him and look after him (for many years, nobody except Cuthbert had been inside). Looking round, he spotted the monk I mentioned before, who suffered from diarrhoea, and he said, "Let Walhstod come in with me" (Walhstod was the monk's name).

'So Walhstod stayed inside with him, until twelve o'clock. As he was going out, he said to me,

"The bishop orders you to come in to him. And I can tell you an amazing thing that has happened to me: as soon as I went in there and touched the bishop, to lead him to the oratory, I felt that I was cured of my long illness."

'Without doubt, this happened because of heavenly mercy. The saint who had cured so many people, cured this monk when he was about to die, to show that a holy man, even when he is sick in body, has perfect health in his soul.

'In this cure, Cuthbert followed the example of the most holy and reverend father and bishop, Aurelius Augustine, who cured a sick man when he himself was dying. This man begged him to lay his hands on him, so that he could be healed. At first the bishop said, "How can I cure you? I can't even cure myself."

'But the sick man said, "I was commanded to visit you: I heard these words in my sleep: Go to Bishop Augustine, so that he can lay his hands on you, and you shall be healed."

'Hearing this, Augustine laid his hand on the sick man, gave him his blessing and then dismissed him, cured, to his own house.

39. 'When I went to Cuthbert at about twelve, I found him reclining in a corner of his oratory, opposite the altar, so I sat down with him. He didn't say much, because the pain of his illness prevented him from speaking easily. But I begged him to leave behind some words which might be like an

inheritance, and a last farewell, to the monks. So he began to speak a few powerful words about peace and humility.

'He warned us against people who wrestle with peace and humility rather than enjoying them. "Keep peace with one another, and heavenly charity, and when you have to discuss things, make sure you all agree on what you decide. Be friendly with other servants of Christ. Don't despise anyone who lives in faith's house, who comes to you, seeking hospitality. Be careful to welcome such people, to entertain them, and send them away with friendly kindness. Don't think you are better than the other followers of the same faith and mode of life.

' "As for people who are not in the Catholic fold, for instance because they don't celebrate Easter at the proper time, or because they live wicked lives, have nothing to do with them.

' "Remember that if necessity forces you to choose one of two evils, I would much rather you dig up the bones from my tomb and carry them away with you, and stay with them wherever God sees fit, than give in to evil and be ruled by people who bring disunity to the church.

' "Strive to learn and to follow the Catholic rules of the Fathers of the Church; and also carefully follow those rules of life which the divine mercy has allowed me to give to you. I know that my life has been contemptible in some people's eyes; but I believe that after my death, you will see what I have been, and that the doctrine I have taught is not to be despised."

'That was the kind of thing Cuthbert said, with pauses in between, because his illness made it impossible for him to speak too much. He spent a quiet day like this, till evening, in the expectation of future blessedness, and at night he stayed awake, calmly praying.

'When it was time for the night-time prayers, Cuthbert received the sacraments from me, and fortified himself for his departure, which he knew was to be soon, with the Body and Blood of our Lord. Lifting up his eyes and hands to heaven, his soul, hungry for heavenly praise, departed to the joys of the kingdom of heaven.

40. 'I immediately went out and announced his death to the monks, who had also passed the night in wakefulness and prayer. At that moment they were chanting the fifty-ninth Psalm, which begins, "O God, you have cast us off and destroyed us: you have been angry, and had mercy upon us."

'One of the monks ran and lit two torches, and holding one in each hand, he went up to a higher place, to show to the monks who remained at the monastery of Lindisfarne, that the soul of Cuthbert had now departed to the Lord (this was the signal agreed beforehand).

'When the monk who was keeping watch on the Lindisfarne watch-tower saw this, he ran quickly to the church, where all the brothers were assembled to sing the night-psalms. It happened that they were singing the same psalm as the monks had been singing on Cuthbert's island. Given what happened later, we must take this as a sign, because after Cuthbert was buried, a violent storm of temptation shook that church, and several monks chose to leave, rather than face such dangers.*

'The year after, Eadberct was made bishop, and because he was a man noted for great goodness and deep learning in the Scriptures, and above all given to charity, he stopped the storm that had arisen. To speak in the words of Scripture, "The Lord doth build up Jerusalem: (that is, the vision of peace) he gathereth together the outcasts of Israel. He healeth the broken in heart, and bindeth up their wounds." [Psalm 147]

'So the meaning of the Psalm which was sung when the death of Cuthbert was announced was made clear: after his death the people would be cast off and destroyed; but after they had experienced the threatened anger of the Lord, they would know heavenly mercy. And whoever carefully reads the rest of the Psalm will see how well it fits this case.

'We put the body of our venerable father in a boat and brought it back to the island of Lindisfarne. It was received by a great crowd of people, together with choirs of choristers, and was deposited in a stone coffin in the church of the blessed apostle Peter, on the right side of the altar.'

* It used to be thought that the trouble alluded to here was an invasion by the Picts, but it seems more

likely it was caused by the cantankerous saint Wilfrid, who briefly had control of Cuthbert's diocese.

V. Life After Death

41. 'But the miraculous cures which Cuthbert performed during his life continued after he was dead and buried. A boy in the neighbourhood of Lindisfarne was troubled by a cruel spirit, so that he went mad and yelled, howled and tried to destroy everything he could reach. He even tried to bite his own limbs. A priest, experienced in exorcism, had been sent to the boy from our monastery, but he could do no good at all.

'The priest told the boy's father to take the boy in a cart to the monastery, and pray to the Lord for him at the relics of the blessed martyrs there. The father did so, but the holy martyrs of God would not work the cure: this was to show how much greater Cuthbert was.

'Meanwhile, the boy who was possessed howled and gnashed his teeth, and struck the greatest horror into everyone who saw and heard him. No one could find a cure; but then one of the priests was told by the Holy Spirit to go alone to the place where the water that had been used to wash Cuthbert's dead body had been poured away.

'The priest took a piece of earth from this place, put it into water, and poured it into the boy's gaping mouth, as he was making a horrible sound. As soon as the water touched him, he stopped crying out, shut his mouth; and closed his eyes, which had been staring, bloodshot and furious. His head and his whole body sank into a deep sleep. He passed the night quietly, and, waking in the morning from sleep as well as from madness, he knew that he had been freed from the devil that had vexed him, by the help of the blessed Cuthbert.

'It was wonderful to see the lad restored to health. He went on a pilgrimage round the holy places with his father. The boy gave thanks for the help of the saints: he had been so mad that he didn't know where he was, or even who he was.

'All the monks who had been standing nearby congratulated him, and he praised the relics of the martyrs on bended knees to the Lord God and our Saviour Jesus Christ. Having now been rescued from the cruelty of the devil, his faith was strengthened, and he returned home.

'You can still see the pit into which the miraculous water was poured; it is a square pit, surrounded by wood, and filled with pebbles. It is near the church in which the body of Cuthbert sleeps, a little to the south. From that time many cures have been performed by these pebbles, or by the earth, with the Lord's permission.'

42. It pleased God to show how Cuthbert, who had performed so many miracles in his life, was still miraculous in death. After he had been dead for eleven years, God inspired the monks to open his

tomb. They expected to find nothing but dry bones and dust, which they intended to put in a chest above the floor of the church.

In the middle of Lent, the monks asked Bishop Edberct for permission to do this, and he agreed to their idea, but commanded that they should do it on the twentieth of March, the anniversary of Cuthbert's burial.

On opening the tomb, the monks found Cuthbert's whole body as complete as if he were still alive. In fact, he was more like somebody who was asleep, because the joints of his limbs were still flexible.

All the vestments that he wore were still clean, fresh and bright. When the monks saw this they trembled with fear, and were practically struck dumb. They hardly dared to look at the miracle which lay before them, and didn't know what to do.

They lifted up the saint's garments to check that his body was still preserved, because they were afraid to touch any clothes that had touched his skin. They hurried away to tell the bishop what they had found.

At this time Edberct happened to be living as a hermit in a place remote from the monastery, surrounded on all sides by the flowing waves of the sea. He usually spent Lent here, as well as the forty days before Christmas, in great devotion, abstinence, prayer, and tears. This was the same island where his venerable predecessor Cuthbert had wrestled in secret for the Lord.

The monks also brought the bishop a sample of the vestments in which the holy body had been wrapped. The bishop gratefully received these gifts, and rejoiced to hear of the miracle. He kissed the garments with great affection, as if Cuthbert were still wearing them.

'Clothe Cuthbert in fresh wrappings,' he said, 'to replace those which you have removed; and then place him in the coffin you have prepared. I know that the place which has been blessed by so great a heavenly miracle shall not remain vacant for long. Anyone whom the Lord allows to rest in that place shall be truly blessed.'

And he added, in his wonder, some words that I once put into verse:

Who can put the actions of the Lord into words?
Who can understand the riches of Paradise? While God,
in His mercy, breaking the bonds of death,
Has granted him eternal life in heaven.
He has clothed his lifeless limbs with honour,
Giving fair promises of endless riches.
How blessed the home which you have prepared for him,
Shining with joyful light.
It is easy for you to command that under the ground,
Gnawing decay will not eat his remains.
Oh you who for three days preserved the prophet Jonah,
Snatching life from the jaws of death!
Oh you who preserved the Hebrew children in the
flames,
So that the Chaldean fire would not tarnish the beauty of
Israel!

Oh you who for forty years renewed your people's raiment,
While they trod an unknown road through the pathless desert!
Oh you who will shape the dust and ashes into limbs,
When the last trumpet will shake the world on its axis!

When the bishop had finished speaking with a faltering voice, crying many tears, the monks did as they had been instructed. Having wrapped the body in a new covering, they laid it in a light chest, and set it to rest on the pavement of the sanctuary.

43. Meanwhile Bishop Edberct, whom God loved, came down with a severe illness. The seriousness of his illness increased every day. He grew worse and worse, and soon died, on the sixth of May. He had never wanted to die quickly, and had longed to die at the end of a drawn-out illness.

They deposited his body in the tomb of the blessed father Cuthbert, by placing the chest which contained the saint's bones over it.

Even now, when people of faith demand them, miracles still happen there. In fact, even the vestments which clothed Cuthbert's body, either in life or in death, have healing power.

44. A member of the clergy belonging to the most holy Bishop Wilbrord-Clement of Frisia came to the monastery from beyond the sea. While he was staying for a few days as a guest, he came down

with a very serious illness, which, by getting steadily worse, reduced him to a hopeless condition.

When he was so overpowered by suffering that he seemed to himself to be suspended between life and death, one Sunday a good thought came to him, and he said to his attendant, 'After mass, take me to pray at Cuthbert's tomb. I hope, by the grace of his intercession, to shake off these torments, either by getting better, or by going to heaven.'

The attendant led the sick man into the church with much difficulty, as he was leaning on a staff. When he got to the tomb, he knelt down, and, bowing his head to the ground, prayed for a cure. No sooner had he done this, than he felt that his body had been filled with so much strength from Cuthbert's body that he easily rose up from prayer. Without the assistance either of his attendant or of a staff to support him, he returned to the guest-house. A few days later, his strength was completely restored, and he continued his journey.

45. In a monastery near Lindisfarne, a young man had lost the use of all his limbs, because of the disease which the Greeks call paralysis. As the abbot there knew that there were skilful doctors in the monastery of Lindisfarne, he sent the poor lad there, begging that if anything could be done for him, they would try it.

The doctors did everything they could, at the command of both their bishop and the abbot, but the boy's illness baffled them. And the disease got worse every day, so that soon his whole body, except for his mouth, was paralysed.

When the doctors deserted him and he lay there hopelessly, he fled to the heavenly Physician, who, when asked faithfully, will help us in our troubles, and heal all our sickness.

The sick young man asked his attendant to bring him one of the miraculously-preserved relics of the body of Cuthbert, because he believed that by its power, and the generosity of the Lord, he would be restored to health.

The attendant talked with the abbot, then took the shoes which Cuthbert had worn in his tomb, and put them on the paralysed feet of the sick man (his paralysis had started at his feet).

He did this at nightfall, at the usual time of going to bed, and immediately the patient fell into a placid sleep. As the silence of the night grew deeper, he began to move his feet one at a time, and his attendants could see these movements. As the healing power of the relics of the saint continued, the cure spread up from his feet into the rest of his body.

When he heard the signal for night prayers, the young man awoke and sat up, and his nerves and all the joints of his body felt strong and painless, thanks to the power of the miracle. He rose up, and stood up in the church all through the night Psalms, or matins, giving thanks to the Lord.

When morning came, he returned to the church, where everyone saw him and congratulated him, and he went round all the holy places, praying and praising his Saviour.

So it was that a young man who was carried to the monastery in a cart, with his whole body paralysed, went home on his own legs, and in sound health, with all his limbs strengthened.

In this context it is delightful to remember the unchanging right hand of God, whose wonders started with the creation of the world, and still shine out.

46. I don't want to miss out another heavenly miracle, which divine mercy brought about near the remains of the holy oratory where Cuthbert used to wage war for God. This miracle could be attributed to the merits of Cuthbert, or to those of his successor, Ethelwald – only God knows. It is reasonable to think that the miracle could be attributed to the united merits of both Cuthbert and Ethelwald, together with the faith of the reverend father Felgeld, who was healed by the miracle.

He was the third person to live at this place, and waged spiritual war there as his predecessors had done. He is now over seventy years old, and waits longingly for the start of the life to come.

After Cuthbert, the man of God, had gone to heaven, Ethelwald lived in Cuthbert's home, on his island. He had been tried and tested in the monastery at Lindisfarne, and was found worthy to rise to the rank of hermit.

He found that the walls of the oratory hadn't been very well put together, and that the stormy winds went straight through the planks.

Cuthbert had looked for the beauty of heaven rather than that of any earthly building, and he used to plug these holes with straw, clay or anything that would serve, so that the weather wouldn't interrupt his prayers.

When Ethelwald took possession of the place, he asked the monks who came to see him to bring him a calf's hide. This he nailed up to stop the violence of the storms, in the corner in which he and his predecessor the blessed Cuthbert would stand or kneel in prayer.

After having lived for twelve years in this place without a break, Ethelwald also entered into the joy which is above.

When Felgeld, the third inmate, began to live on the island, Edfrid, the bishop of the church of Lindisfarne, rebuilt the oratory from its foundations up, because it was falling into ruin.

When this work was finished, many devoted people begged the blessed soldier of Christ, Felgeld, to give them some relic of the holy Cuthbert, who was so beloved of God, or of Ethelwald, his successor. So Felgeld planned to cut up the aforementioned calf's skin and give anyone who asked a small piece of it.

But before he gave it away to other people, he tested it on himself to see what power it might possess. He had been afflicted for a long time with an evil-smelling redness and tumour in the face, which had appeared when he was living with the other monks.

Since he had become a recluse, he took less care of his body, and more care of his soul. He lived a deliberately hard life, and he seldom saw the sun or felt fresh air. This made his tumour get worse, and eventually it filled up the whole of his face.

Fearing that the seriousness of his affliction would force him to give up the life of a hermit, he looked for a cure through the intercession of his predecessors on the island. He put a piece of the calf's hide into water and washed his face with it. Immediately the whole tumour and the foul ulcer which was on it disappeared.

I learned this story from a devout priest of this monastery of Jarrow, who told me that he was well acquainted with Felgeld's face when it was swollen and deformed, and that he had afterwards felt, with his hand through the window, that it was quite clear.

Later, Felgeld himself confirmed that it was exactly as the priest had said, and that, from that time, as long as he remained a hermit, which was for many years, his face was always free from any trouble of this kind, by the grace of Almighty God – He Who cures many who live with sickness, and Who in the life to come, will cure us of every sickness of soul and body.

Then he will satisfy our desires with good things, and crown us for ever in His mercy and loving-kindness.

Amen.

Select Bibliography

Bede: *The Ecclesiastical History of the English People* (trans. Bertram Colgrave), Oxford, 1999

Colgrave, Bertram: *Two Lives of Saint Cuthbert: A Life by an Anonymous Monk of Lindisfarne and Bede's Prose Life*, Cambridge, 1985

Heaney, Seamus: *Beowulf: A New Translation*, Faber, 2002

Hegge, Robert: *The Legend of St Cuthbert: In a Modern English Version by Simon Webb*, Simon Webb, 2009

Simeon of Durham: *A History of the Church of Durham*, Llanerch, 1988

Stenton, F.M.: *Anglo-Saxon England*, Oxford, 1971

Stevenson, Joseph: *The Life of Saint Cuthbert Translated by the Rev. Joseph Stevenson*, Burns & Oates, 1887

Stranks, C.J.: *This Sumptuous Church: The Story of Durham Cathedral*, SPCK, 1973

Webb, J.F.: *The Age of Bede*, Penguin, 2004

Webb, Simon: *Four Famous Northumbrians*, Langley Press, 2011

Webb, Simon: *The Prince Bishops of Durham*, Langley Press, 2011

Webb, Simon: *In Search of Bede*, Langley Press, 2010

Webb, Simon: *In Search of the Northern Saints*, Langley Press, 2011

Willem, David: *St Cuthbert's Corpse: A Life After Death*, Sacristy, 2013

Made in the USA
San Bernardino, CA
26 August 2018